GED® TEST SKILL BUILDER: MATH

RELATED TITLES

GED® Test Skill Builder: Math

GED® TEST SKILL BUILDER: MATH

NEW YORK

Copyright © 2012 LearningExpress, LLC.

All rights reserved under International and Pan-American Copyright Conventions.
Published in the United States by LearningExpress, LLC, New York.

Library of Congress Cataloging-in-Publication Data:

GED® Test Skill Builder: Math.—1st ed.
    p.   cm.
   ISBN 978-1-57685-796-0 (pbk. : alk. paper) — ISBN 1-57685-796-4 (pbk. : alk. paper)
  1. Mathematics—Examinations—Study guides 2. GED tests—Study guides. I. LearningExpress
(Organization)
  QA43.P695 2012
  510.76—dc23

                                        2012008478

Printed in the United States of America

9 8 7 6 5 4 3 2 1

ISBN-13 978-1-57685-769-0

For more information or to place an order, contact LearningExpress at:
    2 Rector Street
    26th Floor
    New York, NY 10006

Or visit us at:
    www.learningexpressllc.com

Contents ▶

INTRODUCTION

This book is designed to help people learn the basic math terms and ideas required in order to do well on the GED® Math exam. For some people who are preparing for the GED® Test, it's been years since they used terms like *integers* and *greatest common factor*. To others, math has always seemed like an alien language with numbers and letters jammed together in confusing patterns. Our goal is to change this and help you understand and get comfortable with various basic math concepts.

This book is not designed to prepare people to take the GED® Math exam. Instead, this book focuses on the necessary math skills needed for that test. Without these basic building blocks of mathematics, it would be difficult for a person to prepare effectively for the GED® Math test, much less earn a passable score. However, once these basic math terms and skills are understood, a person is then on the right path toward learning the concepts needed to succeed on this particular GED® Test.

What This Book Contains

- **The LearningExpress Test Preparation System.** Being a good test-taker can boost anyone's GED® Test score. Many of the skills and strategies covered in this chapter will be familiar to anyone who's taken lots of multiple-choice tests, but there is a difference between "familiar with the strategy" and "excellent at using the strategy." Our goal is to get you into that second category, and the next chapter offers the means to do so.
- **Diagnostic Test.** It's always helpful to see where your math skills stand. Therefore, we recommend taking the diagnostic test before starting on the content chapters. By taking the diagnostic test, you should be able to determine the content areas in which you are strongest, and the areas you might need more help in. To help you do this, we've designed the diagnostic test a little differently than the other two practice tests. For the diagnostic, all the questions for a particular standard are grouped together—all Geometry and Measurement questions are together, for example. This way, when you look over the questions you got right

and what you got wrong, you can also determine what math areas you might want to focus extra attention on.

- **Content Chapters.** These chapters form the heart of the book. Here we cover the basic math terms and concepts. To help you understand all these ideas, every chapter has sample questions, helpful tips, summaries, and explanations of the concepts being discussed. We recommend reading these chapters in order and not skipping around, as many of the concepts in the earlier chapters are built upon in the later chapters.

- **Two Practice Tests.** Once you have a better grasp of the basic math skills, the best thing to do is to put those skills to practice. Both our practice tests are designed to be similar to the real GED® Test Math exam in terms of sections and question types.

Taking these tests under timed conditions will help you gain familiarity with taking a timed math test, and this can help you in your GED® Test preparations. However, if you would prefer to work on the questions untimed in order to focus on mastering the basic concepts of the content chapters, that's not a bad idea, either. Either way is helpful preparation.

Preparing for any test takes time. We know that there are more enjoyable things to do than study basic math skills. However, the math concepts contained in this book will be helpful to you not only during the GED® Math exam, but in your personal and professional life after the test as well.

Good luck, and good studying!

1 ▶ THE LEARNINGEXPRESS TEST PREPARATION SYSTEM

Taking any written exam can be tough. It demands a lot of preparation if you want to achieve the best possible score. The LearningExpress Test Preparation System, developed exclusively for Learning-Express by leading test experts, gives you the discipline and attitude you need to be a winner.

The LearningExpress Test Preparation System

Taking the GED® Math exam is no picnic, and neither is getting ready for it. You want to earn the highest possible score, but there are all sorts of pitfalls that can keep you from doing your best on this all-important exam. Here are some of the obstacles that can stand in the way of your success:

- being unfamiliar with the format of the exam
- being paralyzed by test anxiety
- leaving your preparation until the last minute or not preparing at all

- not knowing vital test-taking skills: how to pace yourself through the exam, how to use the process of elimination, and when to guess
- not being in tip-top mental and physical shape
- messing up on exam day by having to work on an empty stomach or shivering through the exam because the room is cold

What's the common denominator in all these test-taking pitfalls? One word: *control.* Who's in control, you or the exam? The LearningExpress Test Preparation System puts you in control. In just nine easy-to-follow steps, you will learn everything you need to know to make sure that you are in charge of your preparation and your performance on this GED® Test. Other test takers may let the exam get the better of them; other test takers may be unprepared or out of shape, but not you. After completing this chapter, you will have taken all the steps you need to get a high score on the GED® Math exam.

Here's how the LearningExpress Test Preparation System works: nine easy steps lead you through everything you need to know and do to get ready for this exam. Each of the steps listed here and discussed in detail on the following pages includes both reading about the step and one or more activities. It's important that you do the activities along with the reading, or you won't be getting the full benefit of the system. Each step tells you approximately how much time that step will take you to complete.

Step 1: Get Information	(30 minutes)
Step 2: Conquer Test Anxiety	(20 minutes)
Step 3: Make a Plan	(50 minutes)
Step 4: Learn to Manage Your Time	(10 minutes)
Step 5: Learn to Use the Process of Elimination	(20 minutes)
Step 6: Know When to Guess	(20 minutes)
Step 7: Reach Your Peak Performance Zone	(10 minutes)
Step 8: Get Your Act Together	(10 minutes)
Step 9: Do It!	(10 minutes)
Total: 180 minutes	(3 hours)

We estimate that working through the entire system will take you approximately three hours. It's perfectly okay if you work at a faster or slower pace. If you can take a whole afternoon or evening, you can work through the whole LearningExpress Test Preparation System in one sitting. Otherwise, you can break it up and do just one or two steps a day for the next several days. It's up to you—remember, you are in control.

Step 1: Get Information

Time to complete: 30 minutes
Activity: Read the Introduction to This Book
Knowledge is power. The first step in the LearningExpress Test Preparation System is finding out everything you can about the types of information you will be expected to know and how this knowledge will be assessed.

What You Should Find Out
The more details you can find out about the exam, the more efficiently you will be able to study. Here's a list of some things you might want to find out:

- What skills are tested?
- How many sections are on the exam?
- How many questions are in each section?
- How much time is allotted for each section?
- How is the exam scored, and is there a penalty for wrong answers?
- Can you write in the exam booklet, or will you be given scratch paper?

Step 2: Conquer Test Anxiety

Time to complete: 20 minutes
Activity: Take the Test Anxiety Quiz (later in this chapter)

Having complete information about the GED® Math exam is the first step in getting control of it. Next, you have to overcome one of the biggest obstacles to test success: *test anxiety*. Test anxiety can not only impair your performance on the exam itself, but it can even keep you from preparing properly. In Step 2, you will learn stress management techniques that will help you succeed on your exam. Learn these strategies now, and practice them as you work through the activities in this book so they'll be second nature to you by exam day.

Combating Test Anxiety

The first thing you need to know is that a little test anxiety is a good thing. Everyone gets nervous before a big exam—and if that nervousness motivates you to prepare thoroughly, so much the better. It's said that Sir Laurence Olivier, one of the foremost British actors of the twentieth century, threw up before every performance. His stage fright didn't impair his performance; in fact, it probably gave him a little extra edge—just the kind of edge you need to do well, whether on a stage or in an examination room. At the end of this section is the *Test Anxiety Quiz*. Stop here and answer the questions on that page to find out whether your level of test anxiety is something you should worry about.

Stress Management before the Exam

If you feel your level of anxiety is getting the best of you in the weeks before the exam, here is what you need to do to bring the level down again:

- **Get prepared.** There's nothing like knowing what to expect and being prepared for it to put you in control of test anxiety. That's why you're reading this book. Use it faithfully, and remind yourself that you're better prepared than most of the people taking the exam.
- **Practice self-confidence.** A positive attitude is a great way to combat test anxiety. This is no time to be humble or shy. Stand in front of the mirror and say to your reflection, "I'm prepared. I'm full of self-confidence. I'm going to ace this exam. I know I can do it." Say it into a recorder, and play it back once a day. If you hear it often enough, you will believe it.
- **Fight negative messages.** Every time someone starts telling you how hard the exam is or how difficult it is to get a high score, start reciting your self-confidence messages to that person. If the someone with the negative messages is you—telling yourself you don't do well on exams, that you just can't do this—don't listen. Turn on your recorder and listen to your self-confidence messages.
- **Visualize.** Imagine yourself sitting in your first day of college classes, or beginning the first day of your dream job, because you have earned your GED® Test credentials. Visualizing success can help make it happen—and it reminds you of why you're doing all this work in preparing for the exam.
- **Exercise.** Physical activity helps calm down your body and focus your mind. Besides, being in good physical shape can actually help you do well on the exam. Go for a run, lift weights, go swimming—and do it regularly.

Stress Management on Test Day

There are several ways you can bring down your level of test stress and anxiety on test day. They'll work best if you practice them in the weeks before the exam, so you know which ones work best for you.

- **Deep breathing.** Take a deep breath while you count to five. Hold it for a count of one, and then let it out on a count of five. Repeat several times.

You need to worry about test anxiety only if it is extreme enough to impair your performance. The following questionnaire will provide a diagnosis of your level of test anxiety. In the blank before each statement, write the number that most accurately describes your experience.

0 = Never
1 = Once or twice
2 = Sometimes
3 = Often

____ I have gotten so nervous before an exam that I simply put down the books and didn't study for it.

____ I have experienced disabling physical symptoms such as vomiting and severe headaches because I was nervous about an exam.

____ I have simply not shown up for an exam because I was afraid to take it.

____ I have experienced dizziness and disorientation while taking an exam.

____ I have had trouble filling in the little circles because my hands were shaking too hard.

____ I have failed an exam because I was too nervous to complete it.

____ **Total: Add up the numbers in the blanks.**

Your Test Stress Score

Here are the steps you should take, depending on your score. If you scored:

- **Below 3**, your level of test anxiety is nothing to worry about; it's probably just enough to give you that little extra edge.

- **Between 3 and 6**, your test anxiety may be enough to impair your performance, and you should practice the stress management techniques in this section to try to bring your test anxiety down to manageable levels.

- **Above 6**, your level of test anxiety is a serious concern. In addition to practicing the stress management techniques listed in this section, you may want to seek additional, personal help. Call your local high school or community college and ask for the academic counselor. Tell the counselor that you have a level of test anxiety that sometimes keeps you from being able to take an exam. The counselor may be willing to help you or may suggest someone else you should talk to.

- **Move your body.** Try rolling your head in a circle. Rotate your shoulders. Shake your hands from the wrist. Many people find these movements very relaxing.
- **Visualize again.** Think of the place where you are most relaxed: lying on the beach in the sun, walking through the park, or whatever relaxes you. Now, close your eyes and imagine you're actually there. If you practice in advance, you will find that you need only a few seconds of this exercise to experience a significant increase in your sense of well-being.

When anxiety threatens to overwhelm you *during* the test, there are still things you can do to manage your stress level:

- **Repeat your self-confidence messages.** You should have them memorized by now. Say them quietly to yourself, and believe them!
- **Visualize one more time.** This time, visualize yourself moving smoothly and quickly through the exam, answering every question correctly, and finishing just before time is up. Like most visualization techniques, this one works best if you've practiced it ahead of time.
- **Find an easy question.** Skim over the questions on Practice Test 1 until you find an easy question, and answer it. Getting even one question answered correctly gets you into the test-taking groove.
- **Take a mental break.** Everyone loses concentration once in a while during a long exam. It's normal, so you shouldn't worry about it. Instead, accept what has happened. Say to yourself, "Hey, I lost it there for a minute. My brain is taking a break." Put down your pencil, close your eyes, and do some deep breathing for a few seconds. Then, you're ready to go back to work.

Try these techniques ahead of time, and see whether they work for you!

Step 3: Make a Plan

Time to complete: 50 minutes
Activity: Construct a study plan, using Schedules A through D (later in this section)

Many people do poorly on exams because they forget to make a study schedule. The most important thing you can do to better prepare yourself for your exam is to create a study plan or schedule. Spending hours the day before the exam poring over sample test questions not only raises your level of anxiety, but is also not a substitute for careful preparation and practice over time.

Don't cram. Take control of your time by mapping out a study schedule. There are four examples of study schedules on the following pages, based on the amount of time you have before the exam. If you're the kind of person who needs deadlines and assignments to motivate you for a project, here they are. If you're the kind of person who doesn't like to follow other people's plans, you can use the suggested schedules to construct your own.

In constructing your plan, take into account how much work you need to do. If your score on the diagnostic test in this book isn't what you had hoped, consider taking some of the steps from Schedule A and fitting them into Schedule D, even if you do have only three weeks before the exam. (See Schedules A through D on the next few pages.)

Even more important than making a plan is making a commitment. You can't review everything you've learned in middle or high school in one night. You have to set aside some time every day for studying and practice. Try to set aside at least 20 minutes a day. Twenty minutes daily will do you more good than two hours crammed into a Saturday. If you have months before the test, you're lucky. Don't put off your studying until the week before. Start now. Even ten minutes a day, with half an hour or more on weekends, can make a big difference in your score.

Schedule A: The Leisure Plan

This schedule gives you at least six months to sharpen your skills and prepare for the GED® Test exam. The more prep time you give yourself, the more relaxed you'll feel.

- **Test day minus 6 months:** Take the diagnostic test in Chapter 2, then review the correct answers and the explanations. Start going to the library once every two weeks to read books or information about successful reading strategies. Find other people who are preparing for the exam, and form a study group.
- **Test day minus 5 months:** Read Chapters 3 and 4 and work through the exercises.
- **Test day minus 4 months:** Read Chapter 5 and work through the exercises.
- **Test day minus 3 months:** Read Chapter 6 and work through the exercises.
- **Test day minus 2 months:** Use your scores from the chapter exercises to help you decide where to concentrate your efforts this month. Go back to the relevant chapters and reread the information. Continue working with your study group.
- **Test day minus 1 month:** Read Chapter 7. Then, review the end-of-chapter quizzes and chapter review boxes in Chapters 3 through 6.
- **Test day minus 1 week:** Take and review the sample exams in Chapters 8 and 9. See how much you've learned in the past months. Concentrate on what you've done well, and decide not to let any areas where you still feel uncertain bother you.
- **Day before test:** Relax. Do something unrelated to the GED® Test. Eat a good meal and go to bed at your usual time.

Schedule B: The Just-Enough-Time Plan

If you have three to six months before the test, that should be enough time to prepare. This schedule assumes four months; stretch it out or compress it if you have more or less time.

- **Test day minus 4 months:** Take the diagnostic test in Chapter 2, and review the correct answers and the explanations. Then read Chapter 3 and work through the exercises. Start going to the library once every two weeks to read books or information about successful reading strategies.
- **Test day minus 3 months:** Read Chapters 4 and 5 and work through the exercises.
- **Test day minus 2 months:** Read Chapter 6 and work through the exercises.
- **Test day minus 1 month:** Take one of the sample exams in either Chapter 8 or 9. Use your score to help you decide where to concentrate your efforts this month. Go back to the relevant chapters and reread the information, or get the help of a friend or teacher.
- **Test day minus 1 week:** Review Chapter 7 one last time, and take the other sample exam. See how much you've learned in the past months. Concentrate on what you've done well, and decide not to let any areas where you still feel uncertain bother you.
- **Day before test:** Relax. Do something unrelated to the GED® Test. Eat a good meal and go to bed at your usual time.

Schedule C: More Study in Less Time

If you have one to three months before the test, you still have enough time for some concentrated study that will help you improve your score. This schedule is built around a two-month time frame. If you have only one month, spend an extra couple of hours a week to get all these steps in. If you have three months, take some of the steps from Schedule B and fit them in.

- **Test day minus 8 weeks:** Take the diagnostic test in Chapter 2, and review the correct answers and the explanations. Then read Chapter 3. Work through the exercises in these chapters. Review the areas in which you're weakest.
- **Test day minus 6 weeks:** Read Chapters 4 and 5 and work through the exercises.

- **Test day minus 4 weeks:** Read Chapters 6 and 7 and work through the exercises.
- **Test day minus 2 weeks:** Take one of the practice exams in Chapter 8 or 9. Then score it and read the answer explanations until you're sure you understand them. Review the areas where your score is lowest.
- **Test day minus 1 week:** Take the other sample exam. Then review both exams, concentrating on the areas where a little work can help the most.
- **Day before test:** Relax. Do something unrelated to the GED® Test. Eat a good meal and go to bed at your usual time.

Schedule D: The Cram Plan

If you have three weeks or less before the test, you really have your work cut out for you. Carve half an hour out of your day, every day, for studying. This schedule assumes you have the whole three weeks to prepare; if you have less time, you will have to compress the schedule accordingly.

- **Test day minus 3 weeks:** Take the diagnostic test in Chapter 2, and review the correct answers and the explanations. Then read Chapters 3 and 4. Work through the exercises in the chapters. Review areas you're weakest in.
- **Test day minus 2 weeks:** Read the material in Chapters 5 through 7 and work through the exercises.
- **Test day minus 1 week:** Evaluate your performance on the chapter quizzes. Review the parts of chapters that explain the skills you had the most trouble with. Get a friend or teacher to help you with the section you had the most difficulty with.
- **Test day minus 2 days:** Take the sample exams in Chapters 8 and 9. Review your results. Make sure you understand the answer explanations. Review the sample essay outline in chapter 5, and reread the end of the chapter review box.
- **Day before test:** Relax. Do something unrelated to the GED® Test. Eat a good meal and go to bed at your usual time.

Step 4: Learn to Manage Your Time

Time to complete: 10 minutes to read, many hours of practice
Activities: Practice these strategies as you take the sample exams

Steps 4, 5, and 6 of the LearningExpress Test Preparation System put you in charge of your GED® Test by showing you test-taking strategies that work. Practice these strategies as you take the diagnostic test, sample quizzes, and practice exams throughout this book. Then, you will be ready to use them on test day.

First, you will take control of your time on the GED® Test. The first step in achieving this control is to understand the format of the test. The GED® Math exam includes 50 multiple-choice questions, and allows 90 minutes. You will want to practice using your time wisely on the practice tests and chapter quizzes, and trying to avoid mistakes while working quickly.

- **Listen carefully to directions.** By the time you get to the test, you should know how the test works, but listen just in case something has changed.
- **Pace yourself.** Glance at your watch every few minutes, and compare the time to how far you've gotten in the section. Leave some extra time for review, so that when one quarter of the time has elapsed, you should be more than a quarter of the way through the section, and so on. If you're falling behind, pick up the pace.
- **Keep moving.** Don't spend too much time on one question. If you don't know the answer, skip the question and move on. Circle the number of the question in your test booklet in case you have time to come back to it later.
- **Keep track of your place on the answer sheet**. If you skip a question, make sure you skip on the answer sheet, too. Check yourself every five to ten questions to make sure the question number and the answer sheet number match.

■ **Don't rush.** You should keep moving but rushing won't help. Try to keep calm and work methodically and quickly.

Step 5: Learn to Use the Process of Elimination

Time to complete: 20 minutes
Activity: Complete worksheet on *Using the Process of Elimination* (later in this section)

After time management, the next most important tool for taking control of your test is using the process of elimination wisely. It's standard test-taking wisdom that you should always read all the answer choices before choosing your answer. This helps you find the right answer by eliminating wrong answer choices. And, sure enough, that standard wisdom applies to this exam, too. Let's say you're facing a question that goes like this:

9. Sentence 6: I would like to be considered for the assistant manager position in your company my previous work experience is a good match for the job requirements posted.

   Which correction should be made to Sentence 6:
   a. Insert *Although* before *I.*
   b. Insert a question mark after *company.*
   c. Insert a semicolon and *however* before *my.*
   d. Insert a period after *company* and capitalize *my.*
   e. No corrections are necessary.

If you happen to know that Sentence 6 is a run-on sentence, and you know how to correct it, you don't need to use the process of elimination. But let's assume that, like some people, you don't. So, you look at the answer choices. *Although* sure doesn't sound like a good choice, because it would change the mean-

ing of the sentence. So, you eliminate choice **a**—and now you have only four answer choices to deal with. Mark an **X** next to choice **a** so you never have to read it again. Move on to the other answer choices. If you know that the first part of the sentence does not ask a question, you can eliminate answer **b** as a possible answer. Make an **X** beside it. Choice **c**, inserting a semicolon, could create a pause in an otherwise long sentence, but inserting the word *however* might not be correct. If you're not sure whether this answer is correct, put a question mark beside it, meaning, "well, maybe." Answer choice **d** would separate a very long sentence into two shorter sentences and would not change the meaning. It could work, so put a check mark beside it meaning "good answer, I might use this one." Answer choice **e** means that the sentence is fine as it is and doesn't need any changes. The sentence could make sense as it is, but it is definitely long. Is this the best way to write the sentence? If you're not sure, put a question mark beside answer choice **e**.

Now, your question looks like this:

Which correction should be made to Sentence 6?
X a. insert *Although* before *I.*
X b. insert a question mark after *company.*
? c. insert a semicolon and *However* before *my.*
✓ d. insert a period after *company* and capitalize *my.*
? e. no corrections are necessary

You've got just one check mark, for a *good answer.* If you're pressed for time, you should simply mark answer **d** on your answer sheet. If you've got the time to be extra careful, you could compare your check mark answer to your question mark answers to make sure that it's better. (It is: Sentence 6 is a run-on sentence and should be separated into two shorter, complete sentences.)

It's good to have a system for marking *good*, *bad*, and *maybe* answers. We recommend using this one:

X = bad

✓ = good

? = maybe

If you don't like these marks, devise your own system. Just make sure you do it long before exam day—while you're working through the practice tests and quizzes in this book—so you won't have to worry about it during the exam.

Even when you think you're absolutely clueless about a question, you can often use the process of elimination to get rid of one answer choice. If so, you're better prepared to make an educated guess, as you will see in Step 6. More often, the process of elimination allows you to get down to only two possibly right answers. Then you're in a strong position to guess. And sometimes, even though you don't know the right answer, you find it simply by getting rid of the wrong ones, as you did in the previous example.

Try using your powers of elimination on the following questions. The answer explanations show one possible way you might use the process to arrive at the right answer. The process of elimination is your tool for the next step, which is knowing when to guess.

Step 6: Know When to Guess

Time to complete: 20 minutes

Activity: Complete Worksheet on *Your*
Guessing Ability

Armed with the process of elimination, you're ready to take control of one of the big questions in test-taking: *Should I guess?* The first and main answer is *yes*. Unless the exam has a so-called guessing penalty, you have nothing to lose and everything to gain from guessing. The more complicated answer depends both on the exam and on you—your personality and your *guessing intuition*.

The GED® Math exam doesn't use a guessing penalty. The number of multiple-choice questions you answer correctly earn one point each, and you simply do not earn a point for wrong answers. So most of the time, you don't have to worry—simply go ahead and guess. But if you find that a test does have a guessing penalty, you should read the following section to find out what that means for you.

How the Guessing Penalty Works

A guessing penalty really only works against random guessing—filling in the little circles to make a nice pattern on your answer sheet. If you can eliminate one or more answer choices, as outlined previously, you're better off taking a guess than leaving the answer blank, even on the sections that have a penalty.

Here's how a guessing penalty works: Depending on the number of answer choices in a given exam, some proportion of the number of questions you get wrong is subtracted from the total number of questions you got right. For instance, if there are four answer choices, typically the guessing penalty is one-third of your wrong answers. Suppose you took an exam of 100 questions. You answered 88 of them right and 12 wrong. If there's no guessing penalty, your score is simply 88. But if there's a one-third point guessing penalty, the scorers take your 12 wrong answers and divide by three to come up with four. Then they subtract that four from your correct answer score of 88 to leave you with a score of 84. Thus, you would have been better off if you had simply not answered those 12 questions. Then your total score would still be 88 because there wouldn't be anything to subtract.

What You Should Do about the Guessing Penalty

You now know how a guessing penalty works. The first thing this means for you is that marking your answer sheet at random doesn't pay off. If you're running out

Using the Process of Elimination

Use the process of elimination to answer the following questions.

1. Ilsa is as old as Meghan will be in five years. The difference between Ed's age and Meghan's age is twice the difference between Ilsa's age and Meghan's age. Ed is 29. How old is Ilsa?
   a. 4
   b. 10
   c. 19
   d. 24

2. "All drivers of commercial vehicles must carry a valid commercial driver's license whenever operating a commercial vehicle."

   According to this sentence, which of the following people need NOT carry a commercial driver's license?
   a. a truck driver idling his engine while waiting to be directed to a loading dock
   b. a bus operator backing her bus out of the way of another bus in the bus lot
   c. a taxi driver driving his personal car to the grocery store
   d. a limousine driver taking the limousine to her home after dropping off her last passenger of the evening

3. Smoking tobacco has been linked to
   a. increased risk of stroke and heart attack.
   b. all forms of respiratory disease.
   c. increasing mortality rates over the past ten years.
   d. juvenile delinquency.

4. Which of the following words is spelled correctly?
   a. incorrigible
   b. outragous
   c. domestickated
   d. understandible

Answers

Here are the answers, as well as some suggestions as to how you might have used the process of elimination to find them.

1. **d.** You should have eliminated choice **a** right off the bat. Ilsa can't be four years old if Meghan is going to be Ilsa's age in five years. The best way to eliminate other answer choices is to try plugging them in to the information given in the problem. For instance, for choice **b**, if Ilsa is 10, then Meghan must be 5. The difference between their ages is 5. The difference between Ed's age, 29, and Meghan's age, 5, is 24. Is 24 two times 5? No. Then choice **b** is wrong. You could eliminate choice **c** in the same way and be left with choice **d**.

2. **c.** Note the word *not* in the question, and go through the answers one by one. Is the truck driver in choice **a** "operating a commercial vehicle"? Yes, idling counts as "operating," so he needs to have a commercial driver's license. Likewise, the bus operator in choice **b** is operating a commercial vehicle; the question doesn't say the operator has to be on the street. The limo driver in choice **d** is operating

a commercial vehicle, even if it doesn't have a passenger in it. However, the driver in choice **c** is not operating a commercial vehicle, but his own private car.

3. **a.** You could eliminate choice **b** simply because of the presence of the word *all*. Such absolutes hardly ever appear in correct answer choices. Choice **c** looks attractive until you think a little about what you know—aren't fewer people smoking these days, rather than more? So how could smoking be responsible for a higher mortality rate? (If you didn't know that mortality rate means the rate at which people die, you might keep this choice as a possibility, but you would still be able to eliminate two answers and have only two to choose from.) And choice **d** is plain silly, so you could eliminate that one, too. You are left with the correct choice, **a**.

4. **a.** How you used the process of elimination here depends on which words you recognized as being spelled incorrectly. If you knew that the correct spellings were *outrageous*, *domesticated*, and *understandable*, then you were home free.

Your Guessing Ability

The following are ten really hard questions. You are not supposed to know the answers. Rather, this is an assessment of your ability to guess when you don't have a clue. Read each question carefully, as if you were expected to answer it. If you have any knowledge of the subject, use that knowledge to help you eliminate wrong answer choices.

1. September 7 is Independence Day in
   a. India.
   b. Costa Rica.
   c. Brazil.
   d. Australia.

2. Which of the following is the formula for determining the momentum of an object?
   a. $p = MV$
   b. $F = ma$
   c. $P = IV$
   d. $E = mc^2$

3. Because of the expansion of the universe, the stars and other celestial bodies are all moving away from each other. This phenomenon is known as
   a. Newton's first law.
   b. the big bang.
   c. gravitational collapse.
   d. Hubble flow.

4. American author Gertrude Stein was born in
   a. 1713.
   b. 1830.
   c. 1874.
   d. 1901.

5. Which of the following is NOT one of the Five Classics attributed to Confucius?
   a. *I Ching*
   b. *Book of Holiness*
   c. *Spring and Autumn Annals*
   d. *Book of History*

6. The religious and philosophical doctrine that holds that the universe is constantly in a struggle between good and evil is known as
   a. Pelagianism.
   b. Manichaeanism.
   c. neo-Hegelianism.
   d. Epicureanism.

7. The third Chief Justice of the U.S. Supreme Court was
   a. John Blair.
   b. William Cushing.
   c. James Wilson.
   d. John Jay.

8. Which of the following is the poisonous portion of a daffodil?
   a. the bulb
   b. the leaves
   c. the stem
   d. the flowers

9. The winner of the Masters golf tournament in 1953 was
   a. Sam Snead.
   b. Cary Middlecoff.
   c. Arnold Palmer.
   d. Ben Hogan.

10. The state with the highest per capita personal income in 1980 was
   a. Alaska.
   b. Connecticut.
   c. New York.
   d. Texas.

Answers

Check your answers against the following correct answers.

   1. c
   2. a
   3. d
   4. c
   5. b
   6. b
   7. b
   8. a
   9. d
   10. a

How Did You Do?

You may have simply gotten lucky and actually known the answer to one or two questions. In addition, your guessing was probably more successful if you were able to use the process of elimination on any of the questions. Maybe you didn't know who the third Chief Justice was (question 7), but you knew that John Jay was the first. In that case, you would have eliminated choice **d** and, therefore, improved your odds of guessing right from one in four to one in three.

According to probability, you should get two-and-a-half answers correct, so getting either two or three right would be average. If you got four or more right, you may be a really terrific guesser. If you got one or none right, you may be a really bad guesser.

Keep in mind, though, that this is only a small sample. You should continue to keep track of your guessing ability as you work through the sample questions in this book. Circle the numbers of questions you guess on as you make your guess; or, if you don't have time while you take the practice tests, go back afterward and try to remember which questions you guessed at. Remember, on a test with four answer choices, your chance of guessing correctly is one in four. So keep a separate "guessing" score for each exam. How many questions did you guess on? How many did you get right? If the number you got right is at least one-fourth of the number of questions you guessed on, you are at least an average guesser—maybe better—and you should always go ahead and guess on the real exam. If the number you got right is significantly lower than one-fourth of the number you guessed on, you would be safe in guessing anyway, but maybe you would feel more comfortable if you guessed only selectively, when you can eliminate a wrong answer or at least have a good feeling about one of the answer choices.

Remember, even if you are a play-it-safe person with lousy intuition, you are still safe guessing every time.

of time on an exam that has a guessing penalty, you should not use your remaining seconds to mark a pretty pattern on your answer sheet. Take those few seconds to try to answer one more question right. But as soon as you get out of the realm of random guessing, the guessing penalty no longer works against you. If you can use the process of elimination to get rid of even one wrong answer choice, the odds stop being against you and start working in your favor.

Sticking with our example of an exam that has four answer choices, eliminating just one wrong answer makes your odds of choosing the correct answer one in three. That's the same as the one-out-of-three guessing penalty—even odds. If you eliminate two answer choices, your odds are one in two—better than the guessing penalty. In either case, you should go ahead and choose one of the remaining answer choices.

When There Is No Guessing Penalty

As noted previously, the GED® Math Test does *not* have a guessing penalty. That means that, all other things being equal, you should always go ahead and guess, even if you have no idea what the question means. Nothing can happen to you if you're wrong. But all other things aren't necessarily equal. The other factor in deciding whether to guess, besides the guessing penalty, is you. There are two things you need to know about yourself before you go into the exam:

- Are you a risk-taker?
- Are you a good guesser?

Your risk-taking temperament matters most on exams with a guessing penalty. Without a guessing penalty, even if you're a play-it-safe person, guessing is perfectly safe. Overcome your anxieties, and go ahead and mark an answer. But what if you're not much of a risk taker, and you think of yourself as the world's

worst guesser? Complete the worksheet *Your Guessing Ability* to get an idea of how good your intuition is.

Step 7: Reach Your Peak Performance Zone

Time to complete: 10 minutes to read; weeks to complete!
Activity: Complete the *Physical Preparation Checklist*

To get ready for a challenge like a big test, you also have to take control of your physical, as well as your mental, state. Exercise, proper diet, and rest will ensure that your body works with, rather than against, your mind on test day, as well as during your preparation.

Exercise

If you don't already have a regular exercise program going, the time during which you're preparing for an exam is actually an excellent time to start one. And if you're already keeping fit—or trying to get that way—don't let the pressure of preparing for an exam fool you into quitting now. Exercise helps reduce stress by pumping wonderful, good-feeling hormones called *endorphins* into your system. It also increases the oxygen supply throughout your body, including your brain, so you will be at peak performance on exam day.

A half hour of vigorous activity—enough to raise a sweat—every day should be your aim. If you're really pressed for time, every other day is OK. Choose an activity you like and get out there and do it. Jogging with a friend always makes the time go faster, as does running with a radio. But don't overdo it. You don't want to exhaust yourself. Moderation is the key.

Physical Preparation Checklist

For the week before the exam, write down what physical exercise you engaged in and for how long and what you ate for each meal. Remember, you're trying for at least half an hour of exercise every other day (preferably every day) and a balanced diet that's light on junk food.

Exam minus 7 days

Exercise: _____ for _____ minutes

Breakfast: _____

Lunch: _____

Dinner: _____

Snacks: _____

Exam minus 6 days

Exercise: _____ for _____ minutes

Breakfast: _____

Lunch: _____

Dinner: _____

Snacks: _____

Exam minus 5 days

Exercise: _____ for _____ minutes

Breakfast: _____

Lunch: _____

Dinner: _____

Snacks: _____

Exam minus 4 days

Exercise: _____ for _____ minutes

Breakfast: _____

Lunch: _____

Dinner: _____

Snacks: _____

Exam minus 3 days

Exercise: _____ for _____ minutes

Breakfast: _____

Lunch: _____

Dinner: _____

Snacks: _____

Exam minus 2 days

Exercise: _____ for _____ minutes

Breakfast: _____

Lunch: _____

Dinner: _____

Snacks: _____

Exam minus 1 day

Exercise: _____ for _____ minutes

Breakfast: _____

Lunch: _____

Dinner: _____

Snacks: _____

Diet

First of all, cut out the junk. Then, go easy on caffeine. What your body needs for peak performance is simply a balanced diet. Eat plenty of fruits and vegetables, along with protein and carbohydrates. Foods that are high in lecithin (an amino acid), such as fish and beans, are especially good brain foods. The night before the test, you might "carbo-load" the way athletes do before a contest. Eat a big plate of spaghetti, rice and beans, or whatever your favorite carbohydrate is.

Rest

You probably know how much sleep you need every night to be at your best, even if you don't always get it. Make sure you do get that much sleep, though, for at least a week before the exam. Moderation is important here, too. Too much sleep will just make you groggy.

If you're not a morning person and your test will be given in the morning, you should reset your internal clock so that your body doesn't think you're taking an exam at 3 a.m. You have to start this process well before the day of the test. The way it works is to get up half an hour earlier each morning, and then go to bed half an hour earlier each night. Don't try it the other way around; you will just toss and turn if you go to bed early without having gotten up early. The next morning, get up another half an hour earlier, and so on. How long you will have to do this depends on how late you're used to getting up. Use the *Physical Preparation Checklist* to make sure you're in tip-top form.

Step 8: Get Your Act Together

Time to complete: 10 minutes to read; time to complete will vary
Activity: Complete *Final Preparations* worksheet
You're in control of your mind and body; you're in charge of test anxiety, your preparation, and your test-taking strategies. Now, it's time to take charge of external factors, like the testing site and the materials you need to take the test.

Find Out Where the Exam Is and Make a Trial Run

Make sure you know exactly when and where your test is being held. Do you know how to get to the exam site? Do you know how long it will take to get there? If not, make a trial run, preferably on the same day of the week at the same time of day as the real test. Note on the worksheet *Final Preparations* the amount of time it will take you to get to the test site. Plan on arriving 10 to 15 minutes early so you can get the lay of the land, use the bathroom, and calm down. Then, figure out how early you will have to get up that morning, and make sure you get up that early every day for a week before the test.

Gather Your Materials

The night before the exam, lay out the clothes you will wear and the materials you have to bring with you to the test. Plan on dressing in layers; you won't have any control over the temperature of the examination room. Have a sweater or jacket you can take off if it's warm. Use the checklist on the worksheet *Final Preparations* to help you pull together what you will need.

Don't Skip Breakfast

Even if you don't usually eat breakfast, do so on the morning of the test. A cup of coffee or can of soda doesn't count. Don't eat doughnuts or other sweet foods, either. A sugar high will leave you with a sugar low in the middle of the test. A mix of protein and carbohydrates is best. Cereal with milk and just a little sugar or eggs with toast will do your body a world of good.

Step 9: Do It!

Time to complete: 10 minutes, plus test-taking time
Activity: Ace the GED® Language Arts, Reading
exam!

Fast forward to test day. You're ready. You made a study plan and followed through. You practiced your test-taking strategies while working through this book. You're in control of your physical, mental, and emotional state. You know when and where to show up and what to bring with you. In other words, you're better prepared than most of the other people taking the GED® Test with you. You're psyched.

Just one more thing. When you're finished with the test, you will have earned a reward. Plan a celebration. Call your friends and plan a party, or have a nice dinner with your family, or pick out a movie to see—whatever your heart desires. Give yourself something to look forward to.

And then do it. Go into the test, full of confidence, armed with test-taking strategies you've practiced until they're second nature. You're in control of yourself, your environment, and your performance on the exam. You're ready to succeed. So do it. Go in there and ace the test. And look forward to your future as someone who has successfully passed the GED® Test!

Getting to the Exam Site

Location of exam site: _____

Date: _____

Departure time: _____

Do I know how to get to the exam site?   Yes ___   No ___

If no, make a trial run.

Time it will take to get to the exam site: _____

Things to Lay Out the Night Before

Clothes I will wear   _____

Sweater/jacket   _____

Watch   _____

Photo ID   _____

Four #2 pencils and
blue or black ink pens
(if taking the paper-
based test)   _____

Other Things to Bring/Remember

_____

_____

_____

_____

_____

_____

_____

2 ▶ DIAGNOSTIC TEST

CHAPTER SUMMARY
This is the first practice test in this book based on the GED® Math exam. Use this test to see how you would do if you were to take the exam today.

The primary purpose of this diagnostic is to determine your strengths and weaknesses in the four main math content categories. Therefore, the diagnostic is set up a little differently than the two practice tests at the end of this book, which are designed to mimic the real GED® Math test more closely. For the diagnostic you can use a calculator throughout, and this test consists of the following questions and content standards:

Questions 1–12	Number operations and number sense
Questions 13–25	Measurement and geometry
Questions 26–37	Data analysis, statistics, and probability
Questions 38–50	Algebra, functions, and patterns

The answer sheet you should use for the multiple-choice questions is page 23. Then comes the exam itself, and after that, the answer key. Each answer on the test is explained in the answer key to help you to find out why the correct answers are right, and why the incorrect answers are wrong.

After taking the test, review the answers and determine the areas in which you were strongest and the areas in which you missed the most questions.

This way, you can tailor your studying to focus on areas where you might need more help.

You have 90 minutes to complete the entire diagnostic.

1.	ⓐ	ⓑ	ⓒ	ⓓ	ⓔ
2.	ⓐ	ⓑ	ⓒ	ⓓ	ⓔ
3.	ⓐ	ⓑ	ⓒ	ⓓ	ⓔ
4.	ⓐ	ⓑ	ⓒ	ⓓ	ⓔ
5.	ⓐ	ⓑ	ⓒ	ⓓ	ⓔ
6.	ⓐ	ⓑ	ⓒ	ⓓ	ⓔ
7.	ⓐ	ⓑ	ⓒ	ⓓ	ⓔ
8.	ⓐ	ⓑ	ⓒ	ⓓ	ⓔ
9.	ⓐ	ⓑ	ⓒ	ⓓ	ⓔ
10.	ⓐ	ⓑ	ⓒ	ⓓ	ⓔ
11.	ⓐ	ⓑ	ⓒ	ⓓ	ⓔ
12.	ⓐ	ⓑ	ⓒ	ⓓ	ⓔ
13.	ⓐ	ⓑ	ⓒ	ⓓ	ⓔ
14.	ⓐ	ⓑ	ⓒ	ⓓ	ⓔ
15.	ⓐ	ⓑ	ⓒ	ⓓ	ⓔ
16.	ⓐ	ⓑ	ⓒ	ⓓ	ⓔ
17.	ⓐ	ⓑ	ⓒ	ⓓ	ⓔ

18.	ⓐ	ⓑ	ⓒ	ⓓ	ⓔ
19.	ⓐ	ⓑ	ⓒ	ⓓ	ⓔ
20.	ⓐ	ⓑ	ⓒ	ⓓ	ⓔ
21.	ⓐ	ⓑ	ⓒ	ⓓ	ⓔ
22.	ⓐ	ⓑ	ⓒ	ⓓ	ⓔ
23.	ⓐ	ⓑ	ⓒ	ⓓ	ⓔ
24.	ⓐ	ⓑ	ⓒ	ⓓ	ⓔ
25.	ⓐ	ⓑ	ⓒ	ⓓ	ⓔ
26.	ⓐ	ⓑ	ⓒ	ⓓ	ⓔ
27.	ⓐ	ⓑ	ⓒ	ⓓ	ⓔ
28.	ⓐ	ⓑ	ⓒ	ⓓ	ⓔ
29.	ⓐ	ⓑ	ⓒ	ⓓ	ⓔ
30.	ⓐ	ⓑ	ⓒ	ⓓ	ⓔ
31.	ⓐ	ⓑ	ⓒ	ⓓ	ⓔ
32.	ⓐ	ⓑ	ⓒ	ⓓ	ⓔ
33.	ⓐ	ⓑ	ⓒ	ⓓ	ⓔ
34.	ⓐ	ⓑ	ⓒ	ⓓ	ⓔ

35.	ⓐ	ⓑ	ⓒ	ⓓ	ⓔ
36.	ⓐ	ⓑ	ⓒ	ⓓ	ⓔ
37.	ⓐ	ⓑ	ⓒ	ⓓ	ⓔ
38.	ⓐ	ⓑ	ⓒ	ⓓ	ⓔ
39.	ⓐ	ⓑ	ⓒ	ⓓ	ⓔ
40.	ⓐ	ⓑ	ⓒ	ⓓ	ⓔ
41.	ⓐ	ⓑ	ⓒ	ⓓ	ⓔ
42.	ⓐ	ⓑ	ⓒ	ⓓ	ⓔ
43.	ⓐ	ⓑ	ⓒ	ⓓ	ⓔ
44.	ⓐ	ⓑ	ⓒ	ⓓ	ⓔ
45.	ⓐ	ⓑ	ⓒ	ⓓ	ⓔ
46.	ⓐ	ⓑ	ⓒ	ⓓ	ⓔ
47.	ⓐ	ⓑ	ⓒ	ⓓ	ⓔ
48.	ⓐ	ⓑ	ⓒ	ⓓ	ⓔ
49.	ⓐ	ⓑ	ⓒ	ⓓ	ⓔ
50.	ⓐ	ⓑ	ⓒ	ⓓ	ⓔ

Questions

1. Susan has a large granola bar. She gives $\frac{3}{5}$ of it to her friend Mark. Mark gives $\frac{1}{2}$ of his piece to his friend John. What percentage of the original granola bar does John have?
   a. 15%
   b. 30%
   c. 50%
   d. 60%
   e. 80%

2. A young couple is making a rectangular sandbox in the backyard for their children. The wooden frame sits on flat, level ground and measures 8' by 10' by 1' high. They want to fill the box 75% full of sand. How many cubic feet of sand do they need to buy?
   a. 40 ft³
   b. 50 ft³
   c. 60 ft³
   d. 75 ft³
   e. 80 ft³

3. A Web-based map service says it is 617.5 miles from City A to City B. If a person averages 65 miles per hour while driving and makes 3 stops of 30 minutes each, how long will the trip take, in hours?

   Mark your answer in the grid below.

4. The current U.S. yearly gross national income is approximately 1.4×10^{13}, and the current U.S. population is approximately 300 million. What is the average national yearly income per person?
   a. $467
   b. 4.67×10^3
   c. $46,700
   d. 4.67×10^5
   e. 4.67×10^{10}

5. A neighborhood's water bills are proportional to the area of lawn they must water. If neighbor A pays $100/month for his rectangularly shaped lawn, and neighbor B's lawn is twice as long in each rectangular dimension, what is neighbor B's water bill?
   a. $160
   b. $200
   c. $400
   d. $800
   e. $1,600

6. A credit card has a 24% annual interest rate (2% per month). When a payment is missed, the account is charged a $35 fee plus the month's interest on the outstanding balance. If the statement balance is $4,000 and that month's payment is missed, what is the statement balance the following month?

a. $4,035

b. $4,070

c. $4,015

d. $4,115

e. $4,350

7. The ocean erodes the shoreline along the gulf coast at the rate of 6 feet per year. How many years will it take to erode 72 feet of beach?

a. 6

b. 9

c. 10

d. 12

e. 15

8. Sales tax is 8.25%, except for grocery store food, which is exempt from sales tax. In a grocery store someone buys $3.74 worth of vegetables, $5.69 worth of fruit, 2.5 pounds of steak at $4.99 per pound, and 4 spiral notebooks at $0.99 each. How much is the total bill?

a. $18.71

b. $23.70

c. $25.87

d. $26.19

e. $28.00

9. A large-screen TV is purchased with no interest for 6 months, and a 3%-per-month interest after 6 months. The TV costs $1,200, and the person doesn't make any payments for 9 months. Assuming simple interest, how much is owed after 9 months?

a. $1,224

b. $1,236

c. $1,308

d. $1,311

e. $1,524

10. At 6:00 a.m. in the morning the outside temperature is 34 degrees Fahrenheit, and at noon it is a factor of 2.5 times higher. What is the average temperature rise in degrees Fahrenheit per hour between 6:00 a.m. and noon?

a. 0.4

b. 5.7

c. 8.4

d. 8.5

e. 14.2

11. A semi-tractor trailer can carry 40,000 pounds of freight. A company needs to move 187,000 pounds of freight. How many trucks does the company need to hire? (Assume that one truck does not have a full load but that all others do.)

a. 4

b. 5

c. 40

d. 47

e. 50

12. What is 8% of $\frac{1}{3}$ of 99?

Mark your answer in the grid below.

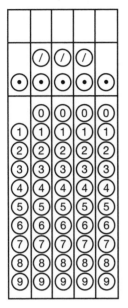

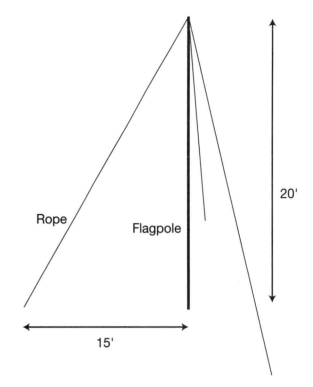

Rope

Flagpole

20'

15'

13. A flagpole is being placed straight up into the ground, and it reaches 20' high into the air. While it is being secured into the ground, three pieces of rope are attached equally spaced around the pole top to stakes in the ground located 15' from the pole base (see above figure). What is the total length of rope needed to span all the lengths?

a. 25 feet

b. 60 feet

c. 75 feet

d. 80 feet

e. 105 feet

Use the following figure to answer questions 14 and 15.

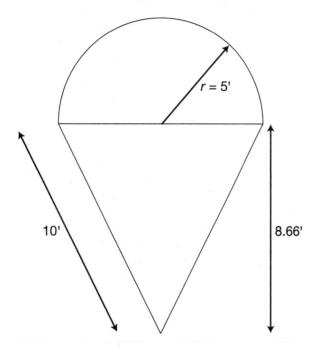

14. A cone-shaped plot of garden has dimensions as shown in the above figure. What is the total area of the garden in square feet?
    a. 39.25
    b. 43.30
    c. 75.55
    d. 82.55
    e. 121.85

15. An edge guard will be placed around the perimeter of the garden. How many feet of edging is needed from the hardware store?
    a. 30.0
    b. 35.7
    c. 39.2
    d. 51.4
    e. 82.6

16. A round swimming pool in a backyard has a 15' diameter and is 4' high. If it is filled to the brim, approximately how many gallons of water does it hold? Water density is 7.48 gallons per cubic foot.
    a. 94
    b. 707
    c. 2,826
    d. 3,965
    e. 5,285

17. Assuming an outdoor water spigot/hose combination can flow water at 5 gallons per minute, about how many hours does it take to fill up the swimming pool described in the previous question?
    a. 8.8
    b. 9.4
    c. 17.6
    d. 18.8
    e. 1,057

18. A farmer owns 80 acres of farmland and grows corn. The average yearly crop yield is 150 bushels of corn per acre. If the current price of corn is $7.11 per bushel, how much money will the farmer receive for his crop?
   a. $1,067
   b. $8,532
   c. $12,000
   d. $84,000
   e. $85,320

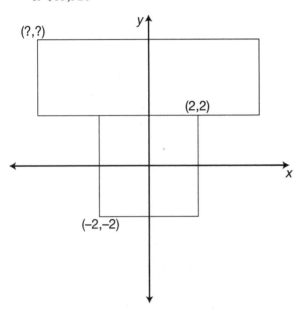

19. A square with sides of length 4 is centered on a coordinate grid. A rectangle of height 3 and width 8 sits symmetrically on top. What is the coordinate of the top left corner of the rectangle?

   Mark your answer on the coordinate grid below.

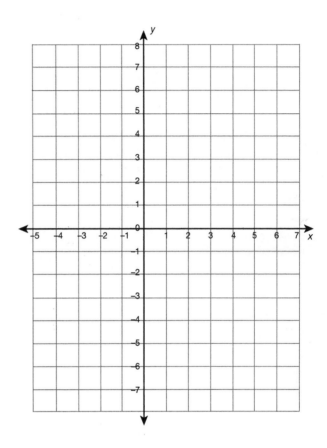

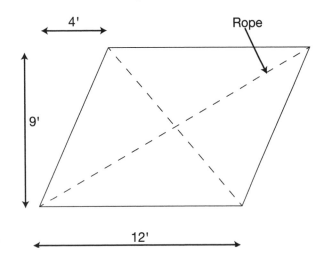

20. A dog pen is being built in the shape of a parallelogram with the dimensions shown above. To support it during construction, two lengths of rope are tied between opposite corners. Approximately how many feet of rope are required to reach between the two pairs of corners?
  a. 21.0
  b. 30.0
  c. 30.4
  d. 40.4
  e. 42.0

21. A large box with dimensions 2' × 3' × 4' needs to be wrapped for a gift. How many square feet of wrapping paper is required?
  a. 24
  b. 36
  c. 42
  d. 48
  e. 52

22. A cylinder is 8 inches in diameter and 8 inches tall. If the diameter is doubled and the height is cut in half, how much larger is the volume?
  a. half as large
  b. the same size
  c. twice as large
  d. four times as large
  e. sixteen times as large

23. A person measures a bedroom for new carpet. The dimensions are $10\frac{2}{3}$ feet by $12\frac{1}{2}$ feet. What is the number of square feet of carpet required? Mark your answer in the grid below.

24. A liquid railcar's carrying capacity is specified as the volume it can carry. Which answer contains only valid volume units?
  a. cubic meters, gallons, cup, acre-feet, cubic inches
  b. cubic feet, kilograms, tablespoons, cubic centimeters
  c. kilograms per cubic meter, acre-feet, teaspoons, bushels
  d. barrels, cups, carats, tons, cubic miles
  e. acre-feet, pounds per cubic feet, cubic feet, barrels

25. A person is paving his backyard patio with standard solid red bricks, which weigh 5.0 pounds each and have standard dimensions $8" \times 2\frac{1}{4}" \times 3\frac{3}{4}"$. The person has a pickup truck with a 1,000-pound cargo carrying capacity. If the bricks are laid snugly together with the largest face showing upward, how many square feet of paved area can be hauled in one load?

a. $36\frac{1}{9}$

b. $41\frac{2}{3}$

c. 150.0

d. 1

e. $1,041\frac{2}{3}$

26. White pine trees are characterized as having a fast growth rate. After one year, a white pine was measured to be 29" tall, after two years 61" tall, at three years 91" tall, and after four years 119" tall. Which of the following is the best assumption for the height of the tree after seven years?

a. 145.0"

b. 146.0"

c. 148.0"

d. 176.0"

e. 208.0"

27. A coin has an equal probability of landing either heads or tails on each flip. The coin is flipped three times in a row. What is the probability that the outcome is all three heads?

a. $\frac{1}{8}$

b. $\frac{1}{4}$

c. $\frac{3}{8}$

d. $\frac{1}{2}$

e. $\frac{3}{4}$

28. A coin has an equal probability of landing either heads or tails on each flip. The coin is flipped three times in a row and results in tails, tails, and heads. What is the probability that on a fourth throw it comes up heads?

a. $\frac{1}{8}$

b. $\frac{1}{4}$

c. $\frac{3}{8}$

d. $\frac{1}{2}$

e. $\frac{3}{4}$

Use the information below to answer questions 29 through 31. There are five houses on the block in a neighborhood. They are priced according to the table below.

House number	Value ($)
1	170,000
2	190,000
3	215,000
4	300,000
5	1,000,000

29. What is the mean house price and the median house price?

a. Mean $215,00; median $215,000

b. Mean $375,00; median $585,000

c. Mean $375,00; median $215,000

d. Mean $215,00; median $375,000

e. Mean $375,00; median $375,000

30. If the owner of house 5 makes additions and landscaping changes that increase his house's value to $1,200,000, what is the new mean and median house price on the block?

a. Mean $215,000, median $215,000

b. Mean $415,000, median $215,000

c. Mean $415,000, median $685,000

d. Mean $215,000, median $380,000

e. Mean $415,000, median $360,000

31. If two new houses are added, one at $190,000 and two at $250,000, what is the mode of the house prices?
 a. $170,000
 b. $190,000
 c. $215,000, $250,000, and $300,000
 d. $170,000 and $1,000,000
 e. $190,000 and $250,000

32. A car buyer is comparing four different models of prospective used cars. Car A sold 27,000 units that year and has a reported 18,000 repair bills averaging $425 each. Car B sold 25,000 units with a reported 16,000 repairs averaging $440 each. Car C sold 30,000 units with a reported 25,000 repairs averaging $370 each. Car D sold 12,000 units with a reported 4,000 repairs averaging $510 each. Which car should someone buy if she wants the lowest expected repair bill?
 a. A
 b. A or B
 c. C
 d. D
 e. B or D

33. There are two six-sided dice: a red one and a blue one. If they are both thrown simultaneously, what is the probability of getting a 3 on the red die and a 4 on the blue die?
 a. $\frac{1}{6} \times \frac{1}{6}$
 b. $\frac{1}{6} \times \frac{1}{6} + \frac{1}{6}$
 c. $\frac{1}{6} + \frac{1}{6}$
 d. $\frac{1}{3} + \frac{1}{4}$
 e. $\frac{1}{6} + \frac{1}{12}$

34. There are two six-sided dice, both red. If they are both thrown simultaneously, what is the probability of getting a 3 and a 4?
 a. $\frac{1}{18}$
 b. $\frac{1}{36}$
 c. $\frac{7}{37}$
 d. $\frac{7}{12}$
 e. $\frac{1}{2}$

35. A cafeteria sells six different sandwiches, three kinds of soups, four different desserts, and eight different beverages. If a person orders a sandwich, a beverage, and a dessert, what is the total number of different possible combinations?
 a. 18
 b. 24
 c. 48
 d. 192
 e. 576

36. A raffle is being held for a school fund-raiser. There are 1,000 tickets, numbered 1 to 1,000. If all the tickets are sold and there is an equal probability for each ticket winning, what is the probability of winning for someone who purchases 6 tickets?
 a. $\frac{1}{1,000}$
 b. $\frac{31}{(1,000 - 6)}$
 c. $\frac{3}{1,000}$
 d. $\frac{3}{500}$
 e. 6

37. Five people are having a foot race. How many different ways could the five people finish the race?
 a. 5
 b. 10
 c. 20
 d. 30
 e. 120

38. Which of the following expressions best represents the following data?

x	value
0	−3
1	−1
2	5
3	15

  a. $3 - 2x^2$
  b. $2x - 3$
  c. $-3x^2 - 3$
  d. $2x^2 - 3$
  e. $3x^2 - 3$

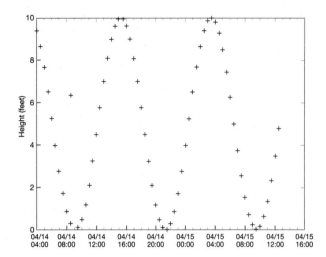

39. What are the values of x and y that solve the following equations?

$$4x + 12y = 8 \text{ and } 3x - 2y = -16$$

  a. $x = -12, y = 4$
  b. $x = 12, y = -4$
  c. $x = -4, y = 2$
  d. $x = 4, y = 2$
  e. $x = -4, y = -2$

40. John is twice as old as Susan. In 4 years John will be 6 years older than Susan. How old are John and Susan now, respectively?

  a. 6 and 4
  b. 8 and 4
  c. 10 and 5
  d. 12 and 6
  e. 14 and 7

41. What is the next value in the sequence?

$1, 3, 3, 9, 27, 243, \ldots$

  a. 27
  b. 270
  c. 6,561
  d. 1,594,323
  e. 1,600,884

42. The tide level in a certain harbor is plotted in the figure above. What is the tide level expected to be at 08:00 on 4/16?

  a. 0.50 ft.
  b. 1.25 ft.
  c. 2.50 ft.
  d. 3.25 ft.
  e. 7.25 ft.

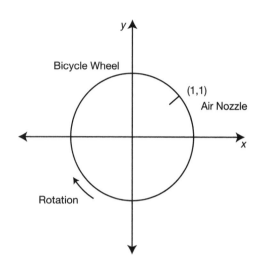

43. A spinning bicycle wheel is centered on a coordinate grid as shown in the preceding figure. At a certain time the air nozzle is as located in the figure. After the wheel spins one quarter of a turn clockwise, what are the new coordinates of the air nozzle?

Mark your answer on the coordinate grid below.

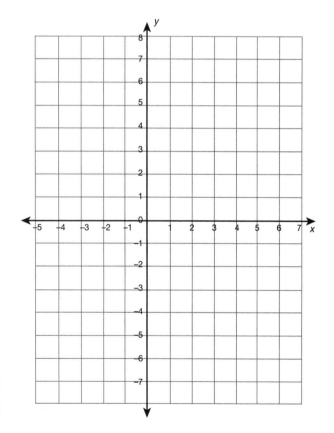

44. In a certain sequence, the next number is always five less than three times the previous number. If the fourth number in this series is 17, what is the sixth number?

Mark your answer in the grid below.

45. A person wishes to exchange U.S. dollars for Euros. At the time, the exchange rate is 1.50 dollars for every Euro. In addition, the exchange center charges a processing fee of $17 before exchanging currency. If a person has m dollars, which of the following equations shows how many Euros that person will receive?

a. $1.5(m - 17)$

b. $\frac{m - 17}{1.5}$

c. $1.5m - 17$

d. $\frac{m}{1.5} - 17$

e. $17m - 1.5$

46. A line has a slope of 4 and a y intercept of -6. What are the coordinates of the line at $x = 3$?

Mark your answer on the coordinate grid below.

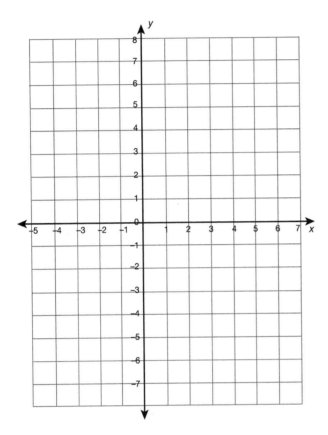

47. What are the values of x that satisfy the quadratic equation $x^2 - 2x - 3 = 0$?
a. -1 and -2
b. 0 and -1
c. 1 and 2
d. 3 and 9
e. -1 and 3

48. A home heating bill is inversely proportional to the outdoor temperature in degrees Fahrenheit, with an increase of $2 in the monthly bill for every degree decrease in temperature. If the monthly bill is $100 when it is 60°F outdoors, what is the monthly bill when it is 50°F?
a. $88
b. $110
c. $120
d. $150
e. $200

49. What are the values of x that satisfy the equation $x^3 = 2x^2 + 8x$?
a. $x = 2, 4$
b. $x = -2, 4$
c. $x = 0, 2, 4$
d. $x = -2, 0, 4$
e. $x = -4, 0, 2$

50. Which of the following equations best describes the following table?

e	f
-3	15
-2	10
1	7
3	15
5	31

a. $f = 3e + 4$
b. $f = 5e$
c. $f = e^2 + 6$
d. $f = 7e - 4$
e. $f = 3e^2$

Answers and Explanations

1. b. The original whole granola bar is 100%, or $\frac{1}{1}$. Taking a fraction means multiplying, first by $\frac{3}{5}$ and then by $\frac{1}{2}$.

$$\frac{1}{1} \times \frac{3}{5} = \frac{3}{5}$$

This is the first step. The next step becomes, "What is half of three-fifths?"

$$\frac{3}{5} \times \frac{1}{2} = \frac{3 \times 1}{5 \times 2} = \frac{3}{10}$$

$$\frac{3}{10} = \frac{30}{100} = 30\%$$

John has 30% of the original granola bar.

2. c. The volume of a rectangular box is given by

Area = $L \times W \times H$.

Area = $L \times W \times H$

Area = $8 \times 10 \times 1$

Area = 80 ft^3

75% full means multiplying the volume by 0.75, or $\frac{3}{4}$.

$80 \times 0.75 = 60$

The couple should buy 60 ft^3 of sand in order to fill the sandbox 75% full of sand.

3. Answer: 11

The formula Distance = Rate × Time is used to get the car traveling time.

Distance = Rate × Time

$617.5 = 65 \times T$

$$\frac{617.5}{65} = \frac{65T}{65}$$

$9.5 = T$

The driving took 9.5 hours, or 9 hours, 30 minutes.

Then the additional 3 stops are added, which total 1.5 hours, or (1 hour, 30 minutes).

$9.5 + 1.5 = 11$

The trip will take 11 hours total.

4. c. The yearly gross national income must be divided by the population for the yearly income per person. The population is 300 with 6 more zeros after it, or 3×10^8 in scientific notation. Division then gives ~$46,700 dollars per person.

5. c. A sketch can be very helpful on this problem. First, draw a rectangle with length of 1 and width of 1. The area of this lawn is A = lw. This is Neighbor A's lawn.

Neighbor B's lawn is twice as long in each dimension, so l becomes $2l$ and w becomes $2w$. The area is now:

$A = lw$

$A = (2l)(2w)$

$A = 4lw$

This area is 4 times as much, and if Neighbor A pays $100, then Neighbor B would pay 4 times as much: 4 × $100 = $400.

6. d. The next month's statement balance will be the previous month's statement balance of $4,000 plus 2% interest on that balance:

$4,000 + ($4,000 × .02) = $4,080.

In addition, there is the $35 fee for missed payment, so the answer is: $4,080 + $35 = $4,115.

7. d. Using the general formula Amount = Rate × Time, the time is just the amount divided by the rate, or $\frac{72 \text{ feet}}{6 \text{ feet per year}} = 12$ years

It will take 12 years to erode 72 feet of beach.

8. d. The total grocery bill is the sum of the groceries, plus the sum of the spiral notebooks AND the 8.25% sales tax on those non-food items. The sales tax adds .0825 to the notebook price, which means multiplying their cost by 1.0825. Therefore:

$3.74 + $5.69 + (2.5 × $4.99) + (4 × $0.99 × 1.0825) = $26.19.

9. c. The simple interest formula is Interest = Principal × Interest Rate × Number of Periods. The interest rate of 3% means .03, and the number of periods is 3 months because the first 6 months had no interest. So the interest owed is $1,200 × .03 × 3 = $108. This amount must be added to the original principal amount for the total amount owed of $1,308.

10. d. The noon temperature is 2.5 times higher, or 85 degrees (34 × 2.5 = 85). Use the general formula: Amount = Rate × Time. The rate of the average temperature rise is the temperature difference divided by the total time:

$$\frac{(85 - 34) \text{ degrees}}{6 \text{ hours}} = \frac{51}{6} = 8.5$$

The average temperature rise is 8.5 degrees Fahrenheit per hour.

11. b. The number of trailers required is the total freight weight divided by the number of pounds each semi-tractor trailer can carry.

$$\frac{187,000}{40,000} = 4.675$$

This must be rounded up to the nearest whole number, 5, since you'll need an entire truck to carry the remaining 0.675 (27,000 lbs.) of the cargo.

12. **Answer:** $\frac{66}{25}$, or 2.64

Multiplying $\frac{1}{3} \times 99$ gives us 33. Next, 8% written as a fraction is $\frac{8}{100}$, or $\frac{2}{25}$ as a reduced fraction, and multiplying that by 33 gives the answer $\frac{66}{25}$. Note that you could also grid in the decimal 2.64, but you cannot grid in the mixed number $2\frac{16}{25}$.

13. c. The pole/ground/rope form a right triangle, with the rope being the hypotenuse. Using the Pythagorean relationship, you can determine the length of rope needed, since it is the hypotenuse of the right triangle.

$a^2 + b^2 = c^2$
$15^2 + 20^2 = c^2$
$(15)(15) + (20)(20) = c^2$
$225 + 400 = c^2$
$625 = c^2$
$\sqrt{625} = \sqrt{c^2}$
$25 = c$

The hypotenuse is 25 feet long, so one length of rope from the top of the flagpole to the ground is 25 feet. There are three of them, so the sum of 3 lengths is 75 feet.

14. d. It is helpful to view this diagram in two parts: there is a semicircle and a triangle. Let's find the area of the semicircle first.
The area of a circle is:
$A = \pi r^2$
$A \approx (3.14)(5^2)$
$A \approx (3.14)(25)$
$A \approx 78.5 \text{ ft}^2$
However, the figure is just a semicircle, or half circle, so its area is $\frac{78.5}{2} = 39.25 \text{ ft}^2$.
For the triangle, the height is given and the base is equal to the diameter of the circle: $2r = 2(5) = 10$ ft. The area is:
$A = \frac{1}{2}bh$
$A = \frac{1}{2}(10)(8.66)$
$A = 43.3 \text{ ft}^2$
Adding $43.3 \text{ ft}^2 + 39.25 \text{ ft}^2 = 82.55 \text{ ft}^2$ for the area of the entire garden.

15. b. The two straight edges of the cone have length 2 × 10 ft. = 20 ft. The semicircular perimeter is half of a circle's circumference:

$C = \pi d$

$C \approx (3.14)(10)$

$C \approx 31.4$

This would be for an entire circle, so we must divide by 2 since it is only a half circle.

$\frac{31.4}{2} = 15.7$ ft.

Adding 20 ft. + 15.7 ft. = 35.7 ft of edging that needs to be purchased.

16. e. The volume of the pool is the area of the circle with radius 7.5 feet multiplied by the height of 4 feet.

$V = \pi r^2 h$

$V \approx (3.14)(7.5^2)(4)$

$V \approx 706.5$ ft^2

Multiplying the volume by 7.48 gallons per cubic foot gives us 5,284.62 gallons.

The swimming pool holds approximately 5,285 gallons of water.

17. c. Using the general formula Amount = Rate × Time, the time required is the volume divided by the water flow rate. However, the answer choices are in hours, and the given flow rate is in minutes, so you should convert the flow rate to hours before dividing. Since there are 60 minutes in an hour:

5 gallons per minute × 60 minutes per hour = 300 gallons per hour

Using the pool's volume of 5,285 gallons (found in question 16):

$\frac{5,285}{300} = 17.6$ hours

It will take 17.6 hours to fill up the swimming pool at the given flow rate.

18. e. The first step to solving this problem is to multiply the crop yield rate in bushels per acre by the number of acres to obtain the total number of bushels produced:

80 × 150 = 12,000 bushels

This number is then multiplied by the price per bushel to calculate a dollar amount:

12,000 bushels × $7.11 = $85,320

The farmer will receive $85,320 for his corn crop.

19. **Answer:** $(-4,5)$

The top of the box is at the line $y = 2$. The top of the rectangle is 3 units higher, or $y = 5$. The rectangle sits symmetrically on top of the square, so it extends 2 units to the left and right of the square $(8 - [2+2] = 4 \div 2 = 2)$. The left side of the rectangle is 2 units to the left of the box at $x = -4$, so the coordinates are $(-4,5)$.

20. c. To solve this problem using equations, you need to see that the diagonals are hypotenuses of two right triangles. If you drew a line straight down from the top right point of the parallelogram and also extended the line that says 12', you would create a right triangle with a height of 9' and a base of 12' + 4' (16' total). The hypotenuse of this right triangle is the longer rope.

$a^2 + b^2 = c^2$

$16^2 + 9^2 = c^2$

$(16)(16) + (9)(9) = c^2$

$256 + 81 = c^2$

$337 = c^2$

$\sqrt{337} = \sqrt{c^2}$

$18.36 \approx c$

The length of the longer rope is approximately 18.36 ft. The shorter rope is the hypotenuse of a right triangle with a height of 9' and a base of 12' − 4' (8' total).

$a^2 + b^2 = c^2$

$8^2 + 9^2 = c^2$

$(8)(8) + (9)(9) = c^2$

$64 + 81 = c^2$

$145 = c^2$

$\sqrt{145} = \sqrt{c^2}$

$12.04 \approx c$

The question asked for the length of rope needed to reach between the two pairs of corners, so we must add the two lengths together: 18.36 + 12.04 = 30.4 ft.

30.4 feet of rope is required to reach between the two pairs of corners.

21. e. To answer this question, it's helpful to draw a diagram or visualize a box, like a shoe box. If you think of this figure, you can see that the box is composed of 6 rectangles. Also, opposite faces of the rectangle are identical, so there are 3 pairs of identical rectangles. The area of a rectangle is length × width, and there are six rectangular surfaces to cover: two of dimension 2' × 3', two of 2' × 4', and two of 3' × 4'. So, $[(2' × 3') × 2] + [(2' × 4') × 2] + [(3' × 4') × 2] = 52$ square feet of wrapping is required to cover the box.

22. c. To answer this question, you need to find the volume of two different cylinders. Fortunately, the formula for the volume of a cylinder is provided on the Formulas Chart.

$V = \pi r^2 h$

$V = \pi(4^2)(8)$

$V \approx (3.14)(4)(4)(8)$

$V \approx 401.92 \text{ in}^3$

This is the volume of the first cylinder. Its diameter is 8 inches, so its radius is 4 inches. In the second cylinder, the diameter—and therefore the radius—is doubled, so the new diameter is 16 inches, and the new radius is 8 inches. The new height is half of 8 inches, or 4 inches.

$V = \pi r^2 h$

$V = \pi(8^2)(4)$

$V \approx (3.14)(8)(8)(4)$

$V \approx 803.84 \text{ in}^3$

The question asks how much larger the volume of the second cylinder is compared to that of the first cylinder. When looking at the volumes, it is apparent that 803.84 in³ (the volume of the second cylinder) is twice as large as 401.92 in³ (the volume of the first cylinder).

23. **Answer:** $\frac{400}{3}$, or 133.33

The area of a rectangle is width × height, so write both dimensions as improper fractions, then multiply and reduce:

$10\frac{2}{3}$ feet × $12\frac{1}{2}$ feet = $\frac{32}{3} \times \frac{25}{2} = \frac{16}{3} \times \frac{25}{1} = \frac{400}{3}$ ft^2.

You could also write this number in the standard grid as the decimal 133.33, but not as a mixed number.

24. a. Even if you do not know what an acre-foot is, kilograms, carats, tons, and pounds are not volume units—they are mass units. Therefore, any answer choice with these units in them can be eliminated.

25. b. First, compute the area of a brick face by using the rectangle area formula length × width. The large brick face is 8" by $3\frac{3}{4}$" = $8 \times \frac{15}{4} = 30$ square inches. However, at this point you must realize that the answer choices are in feet and the brick dimensions are in inches, so you must convert square inches to square feet. A square foot is $12 \times 12 = 144$ square inches, so the large brick face is $\frac{30}{144} = \frac{5}{24}$ square feet.
The carrying capacity is 1,000 pounds, and each brick weighs 5 pounds, so $\frac{1,000}{5} = 200$-brick truck capacity. 200 bricks × $\frac{5}{24}$ square feet per brick = $\frac{1,000}{24} = \frac{125}{3} = 41\frac{2}{3}$ square feet. $41\frac{2}{3}$ square feet of paved area can be hauled in one load.

26. e. Each year, the tree grows about 30 inches. You could create a chart to find its height at year seven.

1	29"
2	61"
3	91"
4	119"
5	(149")
6	(179")
7	(209")

The closest assumption presented as an answer choice is 208.0".

27. a. There are 2 possible outcomes three times, so there are 2 × 2 × 2 = 8 total possible outcomes:

HHH, HTH, HHT, THH, HTT, THT, TTH, TTT

Only one of those outcomes is HHH, so the probability is $\frac{1}{8}$.

28. d. The probability of any single coin flip is independent of any previous or subsequent flips. In other words, it doesn't matter what the previous flip's results are. Therefore, on the fourth flip the coin is still $\frac{1}{2}$ likely to come up heads.

29. c. The mean is the arithmetic average, so adding the five values—$170,000; $190,000; $215,000; $300,000; and $1,000,000—and then dividing by 5 gives a mean house price of $375,000. This means you can eliminate choices (**a**), (**d**), and (**e**). The median is the midpoint between the lowest and highest value when all the values are listed in increasing order, which is $215,000 in this case.

30. b. There are two ways to find the new mean. First, you can simply plug in the new values and divide by 5 again, like you did on the previous question. Alternatively, you can see that the increase in house 5's price is $200,000, and that this increase would be spread over all five houses. The new average price will increase by $\frac{\$200,000}{5} = \$40,000$, so the new mean is $375,000 + $40,000 = $415,000. You can then eliminate choices (**a**) and (**d**). Since house 5 was always the most expensive house (meaning it was nowhere near the middle of this set of numbers), the median is unchanged and remains $215,000.

31. e. The mode refers the number (or numbers) that appear(s) most often in a set. By adding another house valued at $190,000, there are now two houses worth that amount. There were also two houses added that are valued at $250,000, so there are two modes: $190,000 and $250,000.

32. d. The key to this problem is determining the average repair cost per car model. This can be approached different ways. For instance, for Car A you can take the number of repair bills, divide by the number of units sold, and multiply that by the average repair cost:

$\frac{\text{number of repair bills}}{\text{number of units sold}} \times$ (average repair bill)

$= \frac{18,000}{27,000} \times (\$425) = \$283.30$

Multiplying this out for the four cars, the lowest cost is for Car D, with an expected repair bill of $\frac{4,000}{12,000} \times (\$510) = \$170$.

33. a. Rolling two dice are independent events, meaning that the number rolled on the red die has no impact on what number is rolled on the blue die. There are six sides on each die, so there are six possible outcomes for each die. There is only one way to roll a 3 on the red die, so the probability is $\frac{1}{6}$. Likewise, there is only one way to roll a 4 on the blue die, so that probability is $\frac{1}{6}$ also. The probability of rolling a 3 on the red die and a 4 on the blue die when they are thrown simultaneously is $\frac{1}{6} \times \frac{1}{6}$, or $\frac{1}{36}$.

34. a. When rolling two six-sided dice, the total number of possible outcomes is $6 \times 6 = 36$. Die One could be a 3 and Die Two a 4, or Die One could be a 4 and Die Two a 3. In other words, there are two possible outcomes in which a 3 and a 4 are rolled simultaneously. By placing the possible number of desired outcomes over the total number of possible outcomes, you get:

$\frac{2}{36} = \frac{1}{18}$

35. d. Note carefully what the question asks. It does not include soup in the order, only sandwiches, desserts, and beverages. This means you would multiply the following:

(6 sandwiches) × (4 desserts) × (8 beverages)

$= 6 \times 4 \times 8 = 192$

There are 192 different combinations of sandwiches, desserts, and beverages.

36. d. Each ticket has a 1 in 1,000 chance of winning, so 6 tickets give someone a 6 in 1,000 chance, or $\frac{3}{500}$ after the ratio is reduced.

37. e. To answer this, consider the number of people who can finish first: there are 5 initially. After that, the number of people who could finish second is 4, or one less than 5 because you must subtract the person in first place. Going on, the number of people who could finish third is 3, fourth is 2, and last is 1. So, you then multiply these values:

$5 \times 4 \times 3 \times 2 \times 1 = 120$

There are 120 possible ways that the five people could finish the race.

38. d. At $x = 0$ the expression must equal -3, based on the first set of data in the table. This rules out answer choice **a**, since $3 - 2x^2 = 3$ when $x = 0$. The values of $x = 0$ and $x = 1$ work for choice **b**, but be careful—the values stop working from $x = 2$. The values increase as x increases, and this rules out choice **c**, since the negative sign in front of the $3x^2$ would lead to decreasing values. Trying the values for $x = 1$ and $x = 2$ shows that only **d** fits the numbers. Choice **e** is only true when $x = 0$.

39. c. There are two ways to solve this question. The simplest method is to take the values in the answer choices and try them in the equations. Only one set of values will work. While this may require some time, if you use process of elimination as you go along, you may find it doesn't take as long as you might have initially thought.

Another way to solve it is to rearrange one equation and then place that equation into the other. This will be done to solve for one of the variables. For example, the first equation can be changed like this:

$4x + 12y = 8$

$4x + 12y - 12y = 8 - 12y$

$4x = 8 - 12y$

$\frac{4x}{4} = \frac{8 - 12y}{4}$

$x = 2 - 3y$

You can then take this value of x and substitute it into the second equation for x to solve for y:

$3x - 2y = -16$

$3(2 - 3y) - 2y = -16$

$6 - 9y - 2y = -16$

$6 - 11y = -16$

$6 - 6 - 11y = -16 - 6$

$-11y = -22$

$\frac{-11y}{-11} = \frac{-22}{-11}$

$y = 2$

Knowing that $y = 2$ eliminates choices **a**, **b**, and **e**. Placing the value of $y = 2$ into $x = 2 - 3y$ gives you $x = -4$, choice **c**.

40. d. Write two equations for John and Susan's ages: one equation for now and the other equation for 4 years later. If J is John's current age and S is Susan's current age, then J = 2S. In 4 years, John's age will be J + 4 and Susan's will be S + 4, so:

$J + 4 = (S + 4) + 6$

$J + 4 = S + 10$

$J + 4 - 4 = S + 10 - 4$

$J = S + 6$

You can then substitute this value into the first equation for J:

$J = 2S$

$S + 6 = 2S$

$S - S + 6 = 2S - S$

$6 = S$

So Susan is 6, and since John is twice her age, John is 12.

41. c. Each number is formed by multiplying the two previous numbers. Therefore, the next number would be:

$27 \times 243 = 6,561$

42. a. By seeing what the tide level is at 08:00 on the two previous days, you can figure out where it is expected to be on 4/16. On 4/14 at 08:00, the tide level is closer to 0 than 2, so it is probably somewhere just less than 1. On the next day at 08:00, it is a bit lower, maybe 0.75 or less. By 4/16, then, the answer choice that makes the most sense is 0.50 ft.

43. **Answer:** $(1, -1)$

The nozzle at $(1,1)$ is rotated clockwise by one quarter turn, which reflects it across the x-axis, so the new coordinates are $(1, -1)$.

44. **Answer:** 133

Another way to write "the next number is always five less than three times the previous number" is:

$N = 3P - 5$, where N is the next number and P is the previous number. Since the question tells you that $P = 17$, when you place this value into the above equation, you get:

$N = 3P - 5$

$N = 3(17) - 5$

$N = 51 - 5$

$N = 46$

46 is the fifth number in the series, so plug that number into the same equation to get the sixth number:

$N = 3P - 5$

$N = 3(46) - 5$

$N = 138 - 5$

$N = 133$

The sixth number in the series is 133.

45. b. Before the currency is exchanged, the processing fee must be accounted for, so $(m - 17)$ is the first part of the equation. 1.50 dollars gives you 1 Euro, so divide m by 1.5 to convert dollars to Euros.

46. **Answer:** (3,6)

The equation for the line is $y = 4x - 6$, showing a slope of 4 and a y-intercept of -6. Plugging in 3 for x gives $y = 6$, so the coordinates are (3,6).

47. e. Notice that there are negative values in the initial equation. This means choices **c** and **d** can be eliminated since they have no negative values, and there is no way to create negative numbers when all you are adding and multiplying together are positive numbers. If $x = 0$, then you would get $-3 = 0$, so **b** cannot be the right answer. Try the values in choices **a** and **e**, and you will see that only $x = -1$ and $x = 3$ make the equation equal to 0, so choice (**e**) is correct.

48. c. Although the phrase "inversely proportional" sounds like a mouthful, it really only means that one value decreases when another value increases, and vice versa. In this problem, every degree drop in temperature leads to a $2 increase in the heating bill. Since the temperature drops 10 degrees ($60 - 50 = 10$), the heating bill must increase by ($2)(10) = $20, rising from $100 to $120.

49. d. If x is zero, the equation is satisfied, so it is a solution. This means choices **a** and **b** can be eliminated. If x is not zero, then the equation can be divided by x and becomes $x^2 = 2x + 8$. Trying different values from the answer choices shows that $x = -2$ and $x = 4$ satisfy the equation, making choice **d** correct.

50. c. Notice how the values of f decrease as negative e approaches zero, and then increase again as positive e moves away from 0. The best explanation for this is that e is squared, since any number squared is always positive. This eliminates all choices except **c** and **e**, and only choice **c** works with the values listed.

CHAPTER 3

NUMBER SENSE AND OPERATIONS

CHAPTER SUMMARY

In this chapter, you will learn the basics of understanding numbers and how to work with them. You will learn about place value, operations on whole numbers and decimals, fractions, mixed numbers, decimals, percentages, ratios, and proportions.

This chapter covers the basics of numbers and operations. Basic problem solving in mathematics is rooted in number facts. Your ability to work with numbers depends on how quickly and accurately you can understand what numbers mean and do simple mathematical computations.

Place Value

Whole numbers and decimals are made up of **digits**. Each digit has a value, depending on its relative location to other digits. For instance, we know that $365 is not made up of $3, $6, and $5. Instead, we could have 3 one hundred dollar bills, 6 ten dollar bills, and 5 one dollar bills. In other words, the 3 has a value of 3 hundreds, the 6 has a value of 6 tens, and the 5 has a value of 5 ones. We can use a place value chart, like the one in the following example, to help us find the value of the digits in a number.

Example 1: What is the value of the 3 in $4,827.35?

Write the digits and the decimal point (.) in a place value chart. Place the whole number part to the left of the decimal point. Place the decimal part to the right of the decimal point.

Ten Thousands 10,000	Thousands 1,000	Hundreds 100	Tens 10	Ones 1	.	Tenths 0.1	Hundredths 0.01	Thousandths 0.001
	4	8	2	7	.	3	5	

Answer: The 3 is in the tenths place, so it has a value of 3 tenths, or 0.3.

Example 2: What is 13.682 written in word form?

Write the whole number part in word form. Use the word "and" to represent the decimal point. The last digit of the decimal is in the thousandths place, so we use "thousandths" as the value of the decimal.

thirteen → 13.682 ← six hundred eighty-two
      ↑   thousands
    and

Answer: 13.682 in word form is "thirteen and six hundred eighty-two thousandths."

Comparing and Ordering Whole Numbers and Decimals

To compare and order numbers, we compare the digits that have the same place value.

Example: Order 102.37, 145, and 37.5 from least to greatest.

Line up the digits by their place values, using the decimals as a center line. Add zeros so that all the numbers have digits in the same decimal places.

102.37
145.00 ← add decimal point and 0s
37.50 ← add 0

Compare the digits in the largest place value: 0 hundreds is less than 1 hundred, so 37.5 is less than 102.37 and 145.

0 hundreds < 1 hundred
↓
[1]02.37
[1]45.00
[0]37.50

Compare 102.37 and 145 by comparing the digits in the next place value: 0 tens is less than 4 tens, so 102.37 < 145.

0 tens < 4 tens
↓
1[0]2.37
1[4]5.00

Answer: The order from least to greatest is 37.5, 102.37, and 145.

Rounding Whole Numbers and Decimals

Rounding gives us a number that is close to the exact number. For example, if an item costs $17.99, we could say the item costs about $18.00. We could also say the item costs about $20.00. In the first case, we rounded 17.99 to the nearest whole dollar. In the second case, we rounded 17.99 to the nearest multiple of ten dollars (in other words, to the nearest tens).

Example 1: Round 412.33 to the nearest whole number.

Whole number is another way of saying *ones place*. Recall how we got rid of the cents (parts of a dollar) in $17.99 so that we would be left with only whole dollars. Think of decimal digits as parts of whole numbers—to round to a whole number is to eliminate the decimal part.

Identify the digit in the ones place and underline the digit to its right. Any other digits to the right can be dismissed.

$$\text{ones}$$
$$\downarrow$$
$$4\,1\,2\,.\,\underline{3}\,\cancel{3}$$

The underlined digit is less than 5, so we *round down*—this means that our final value will be less than the original number, so the digit in the ones place stays the same. (In other words, 412.3 is closer in value to 412 than to 413.) The underlined digit can now be ignored.

$$\text{ones}$$
$$\downarrow$$
$$4\,1\,2\,.\,\cancel{3}$$

Answer: 412.33 rounded to the nearest whole number is 412.

Example 2: Round 75.359 to the nearest tens.

Identify the digit in the tens place and underline the digit to its right. Dismiss the other digits to the right.

$$\text{tens}$$
$$\downarrow$$
$$7\,\underline{5}\,.\,\cancel{359}$$

The underlined digit is greater than or equal to 5, so we *round up*—this means that our final value will be more than the original number, so the digit in the tens place increases by 1. (In other words, 75 is closer in value to 80 than to 70.) Change the underlined digit to a zero.

$$\overset{8}{\cancel{7}}\ \overset{0}{\underline{\cancel{5}}}$$

Answer: 75.359 rounded to the nearest tens is 80.

Regrouping

We can rename the place value of a digit by **regrouping**. For example, if we have one ten dollar bill, we can trade it for 10 one dollar bills. We still have $10, but we now have one dollar bills instead of ten dollar bills. In other words, we *regrouped* the ten into ones.

Example 1: Regroup two hundreds.

Visualize two hundreds as 2 one hundred dollar bills. To regroup, trade 1 one hundred dollar bill for 10 ten dollar bills. We now have 1 one hundred dollar bill and 10 ten dollar bills.

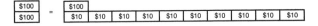

Answer: 2 hundreds = 1 hundred and 10 tens

Example 2: Regroup 11 tenths.

Because 10 dimes equal $1, we can use dimes to represent tenths. Visualize 11 tenths as 11 dimes. To regroup 11 dimes, trade 10 dimes for 1 one dollar bill. We now have 1 one dollar bill and one dime.

Answer: 11 tenths = one and one tenth

In the next section, we will use place values and regrouping to help us perform operations on whole numbers and decimals.

Operations on Whole Numbers and Decimals

The four types of operations are **addition**, **subtraction**, **multiplication**, and **division**.

Addition and Subtraction

When we add and subtract, we always begin with the digits in the *smallest place value*.

Example 1: Add: 62.83 + 45.19

Line up the decimal point and the digits by their place values.

Add the digits in the smallest place value.

3 hundredths + 9 hundredths = 12 hundredths
Regroup: 12 hundredths = 1 tenth and 2 hundredths

Write the 1 in the tenth place and the 2 in the hundredths place.

$$62.\overset{1}{8}3 \rightarrow \quad 6 \text{ tens } 2 \text{ ones } \cdot \overset{1 \text{ tenth}}{8} \text{tenths } 3 \text{ hundredths}$$
$$+ 45.19 \rightarrow + 4 \text{ tens } 5 \text{ ones } \cdot 1 \text{ tenth } 9 \text{ hundredths}$$
$$2 \qquad\qquad\qquad\qquad\qquad 2 \text{ hundredths}$$

Add the digits in the next place value.

1 tenth + 8 tenths + 1 tenth = 10 tenths
Regroup: 10 tenths = 1 one and 0 tenths

Write the 1 in the ones place and the 0 in the tenths place

$$62.\overset{1\ 1}{8}3 \rightarrow \quad 6 \text{ tens } \overset{1 \text{ one}}{2} \text{ ones } \cdot \overset{1 \text{ tenth}}{8}\text{tenths } 3 \text{ hundredths}$$
$$+ 45.19 \rightarrow + 4 \text{ tens } 5 \text{ ones } \cdot 1 \text{ tenth } 9 \text{ hundredths}$$
$$02 \qquad\qquad\qquad\qquad\qquad\quad 0 \text{ tenths } 2 \text{ hundredths}$$

Add the remaining digits. Place the decimal point so that it lines up with the other decimal points.

$$62.\overset{1\ 1}{8}3 \rightarrow \quad 6 \text{ tens } \overset{1 \text{ ones}}{2} \text{ ones } \cdot \overset{1 \text{ tenth}}{8} \text{ tenths } 3 \text{ hundredths}$$
$$+ 45.19 \rightarrow + 4 \text{ tens } 5 \text{ ones } \cdot 1 \text{ tenth } 9 \text{ hundredths}$$
$$108.02 \qquad 10 \text{ tens } 8 \text{ ones } \cdot 0 \text{ tenths } 2 \text{ hundredths}$$

Answer: 62.83 + 45.19 = 108.02

Example 2: Subtract: 482 − 72.50

Line up the digits by their place values. Add zeros to decimal places as needed.

Subtract the digits in the smallest place value.

$$482.00 \rightarrow \quad 4 \text{ hundreds } 8 \text{ tens } 2 \text{ ones} \cdot 0 \text{ tenths } 0 \text{ hundredths}$$
$$- 72.50 \rightarrow - 0 \text{ hundreds } 7 \text{ tens } 2 \text{ ones} \cdot 5 \text{ tenths } 0 \text{ hundredths}$$
$$0 \qquad\qquad\qquad\qquad\qquad\qquad 0 \text{ hundredths}$$

To subtract the digits in the next place value, we first need to regroup.

We cannot take 5 tenths away from 0 tenths, so regroup.

2 ones = 1 one and 10 tenths
Add: 10 tenths + 0 tenths = 10 tenths

We can take 5 tenths away from 10 tenths, so subtract.

10 tenths − 5 tenths = 5 tenths

$$4\ 8\ \overset{\overset{1}{}\ \overset{10}{}}{2}.\cancel{0}\ 0 \rightarrow \quad 4\text{ hundreds}\quad 8\text{ tens}\quad \overset{1\text{ one}}{\cancel{2\text{ ones}}}\ \cdot\ \overset{10+0\text{ tenths}}{\cancel{0\text{ tenths}}}\quad 0\text{ hundredths}$$
$$-\ \ 7\ 2.5\ 0 \rightarrow \underline{-\ 0\text{ hundreds}\quad 7\text{ tens}\quad 2\text{ ones}\ \cdot\ \ 5\text{ tenths}\quad 0\text{ hundredths}}$$
$$\qquad\ \ 5\ 0 \qquad\qquad\qquad\qquad\qquad\qquad\qquad\qquad 5\text{ tenths}\quad 0\text{ hundredths}$$

We cannot take 2 ones away from 1 one, so regroup.

8 tens = 7 tens and 10 ones
Add: 10 ones + 1 one = 11 ones

We can take 2 ones away from 11 ones, so subtract.

11 ones − 2 ones = 9 ones

Subtract the remaining digits. Line up the decimal point.

$$4\ \overset{\overset{7}{}\ \overset{11}{}\ \overset{10}{}}{8\ 2}.\cancel{0}\ 0 \rightarrow \quad 4\text{ hundreds}\quad \overset{7\text{ tens}}{\cancel{8\text{ tens}}}\quad \overset{10+1\text{ ones}}{\cancel{2\text{ ones}}}\ \cdot\ \overset{10\text{ tenths}}{\cancel{0\text{ tenths}}}\quad 0\text{ hundredths}$$
$$-\ \ 7\ 2.5\ 0 \rightarrow \underline{-\ 0\text{ hundreds}\quad 7\text{ tens}\quad 2\text{ ones}\ \cdot\ \ 5\text{ tenths}\quad 0\text{ hundredths}}$$
$$4\ 0\ 9.5\ 0 \qquad\qquad 4\text{ hundreds}\quad 0\text{ tens}\quad 9\text{ ones}\ \cdot\ \ 5\text{ tenths}\quad 0\text{ hundredths}$$

Answer: 482 − 72.50 = 409.50

Multiplication and Division

When we multiply and divide, we can rewrite the decimal numbers as whole numbers by simply ignoring the decimal point. Then we add back the decimal point as the final step.

Example 1: Multiply: $1.25 × 32

Rewrite the decimal number as a whole number.

125 × 32

Line up the digits by their place value.

The number 32 is the same as 30 + 2, so 125 × 32 is the same as multiplying by 30 and multiplying by 2, then adding the products.

We start by multiplying 125 by 2.

Multiply: 2 × 5 ones = 10 ones
Regroup: 10 ones = 1 ten and 0 ones

$$\overset{1}{125} \rightarrow \quad 1\text{ hundred}\quad \overset{\overset{1}{}\ \text{tens}}{2}\quad 5\text{ ones}$$
$$\underline{\times\ 32} \rightarrow \underline{\qquad\qquad\qquad\qquad \times\ 3\boxed{2}}$$
$$\quad 0 \qquad\qquad\qquad\qquad\qquad\qquad 0\text{ ones}$$

Multiply: 2 × 2 tens = 4 tens

Add: 4 tens + 1 ten = 5 tens

$\overset{1}{125} \rightarrow$ 1 hundred $\overset{1}{\underset{}{2}} \overset{tens}{}$ tens 5 ones

$\underline{\times\ 32} \rightarrow \underline{\hspace{4cm}} \times 3\boxed{2}$

50   5 tens   0 ones

Multiply the remaining digit by 2.

$\overset{1}{125} \rightarrow$ 1 hundred $\overset{1}{\underset{}{2}} \overset{tens}{}$ tens 5 ones

$\underline{\times\ 32} \rightarrow \underline{\hspace{4cm}} \times 3\boxed{2}$

250   2 hundreds   5 tens   0 ones

Now we multiply each digit in 125 by 30. There is a special pattern we can follow when we multiply by a number that ends in 0. We multiply by the digit that is greater than 0 and then add 0s at the end. For example:

$125 \times 3 = 375$

$125 \times 30 = 3{,}750 \leftarrow$ Multiply: $125 \times 3 = 375$. There is one 0 in 30, so add one 0 after 375.

$125 \times 300 = 37{,}500 \leftarrow$ Multiply: $125 \times 3 = 375$. There are two 0s in 300, so add two 0s after 375.

Multiply: $125 \times 30 = 3{,}750$

Line up the digits in 250 and 2,750 by place value and add.

$$\begin{array}{r} 125 \\ \times\ 32 \\ \hline 250 \\ +3{,}750 \\ \hline 4{,}000 \end{array}$$

Count the total number of decimal places in 1.25 and 32 to get the number of decimal places in the answer.

$$\begin{array}{l} 1.25 \leftarrow 2 \text{ decimal places} \\ \underline{\times\ 32} \leftarrow 0 \text{ decimal places} \\ 40.00 \leftarrow \text{ total of 2 decimal places} \end{array}$$

Answer: $\$1.25 \times 32 = \$40.00$

Example 2: Divide: $3.52 \div 1.1$

Rewrite 1.1 as a whole number by moving the decimal point one place to the right. Move the decimal point in 3.52 the same number of places to the right.

$$1.1\overline{)3.52} \rightarrow 11\overline{)35.2}$$
$$\rightarrow \quad \rightarrow$$

The first digit in 35.2 is 3, so we must find how many 11s we can put into 3. Think: $11 \times \boxed{?}$ is less than or equal to 3. In this case, no 11s can fit into 3. Multiply and then subtract.

$$\begin{array}{r} \boxed{0} \\ 11\overline{)35.2} \\ \underline{-0} \\ 3 \end{array}$$

$\leftarrow$ Multiply: $11 \times 0 = 0$

$\leftarrow$ Subtract: $3 - 0 = 3$

Bring down the next digit, 5, to get 35. How many times can 11 go into 35? Think: $11 \times \boxed{?}$ is less than or equal to 35. In this case, 11 can go into 35 three times. Multiply and then subtract.

$$\begin{array}{r} 0\boxed{3} \\ 11\overline{)35.2} \\ \underline{-0}\downarrow \\ 35 \\ \underline{-33} \leftarrow \text{Multiply: } 11 \times 3 \\ 2 \leftarrow \text{Subtract: } 35 - 33 \end{array}$$

Bring down the last digit, 2, to get 22. Think: $11 \times \boxed{?}$ is less than or equal to 22. Multiply and then subtract.

$$\begin{array}{r} 0\,3\boxed{2} \\ 11\overline{)35.\,2} \\ \underline{-0}\downarrow \\ 35\downarrow \\ \underline{-33}\downarrow \\ 2\,2 \\ \underline{-2\,2} \leftarrow \text{Multiply: } 11 \times 2 \\ 0 \leftarrow \text{Subtract: } 22 - 22 \end{array}$$

Line up the decimal point in the answer with the decimal point in 35.2

$$\begin{array}{r} 03.2 \\ 11\overline{)35.2} \end{array}$$

Answer: $3.52 \div 1.1 = 3.2$

Powers and Exponents

We use **exponents** to show how many times a number is multiplied by itself. For example, 5^3 is the same as $5 \times 5 \times 5$. The number 5 is called the **base**. The number 3 is the exponent, and it tells us to multiply the base by itself three times. Another name for the exponent is **power**. We read 5^3 as *5 to the third power* or *5 cubed*.

Example 1: Evaluate: 3^4

We read 3^4 as *3 to the fourth power*. The exponent is 4, so we multiply 3 by itself four times.

$$3^4 = \underbrace{3 \times 3}_{9} \times \underbrace{3 \times 3}_{9} = 81$$

Answer: $3^4 = 81$

Example 2: Evaluate: $5^2 \times 2^2$

We read 5^2 as *5 to the second power* or *5 squared* and 2^2 as *2 to the second power* or *2 squared*.

$$5^2 \times 2^2 = \underbrace{5 \times 5}_{25} \times \underbrace{2 \times 2}_{4} = 100$$

Answer: $5^2 \times 2^2 = 100$

Square Roots

Taking a square root of a number is the opposite of squaring a number. The symbol for square root is $\sqrt{}$. We read $\sqrt{49}$ as *square root of 49*.

Example 1: Evaluate: $\sqrt{49}$

Think: What number times itself is 49?

$$\boxed{?}^2 = \boxed{7}^2 = \boxed{7} \times \boxed{7} = 49$$

Answer: $\sqrt{49} = 7$

We say that 49 is a **perfect square** because there is a whole number (7) that will make the equation $\boxed{?}^2 = 49$ true.

Example 2: Evaluate: $\sqrt{15}$

There is no whole number that will make the equation $\boxed{?}^2 = 15$ true, so 15 is *not* a perfect square. To find $\sqrt{15}$, we look for the two closest perfect squares. The two closest perfect squares are 9 and 16.

$$\sqrt{9} = 3 \qquad \sqrt{15} = \boxed{?} \qquad \sqrt{16} = 4$$

Answer: $\sqrt{15}$ is between 3 and 4

Scientific Notation

Scientific notation is a way of writing very large and very small numbers using decimals and powers of 10. A power of 10 is an exponent that has 10 as its base.

Example 1: Write 7.81×10^3 in standard form.

The power of 10 is 3, so we move the decimal point in 7.81 three places to the right, adding zeros as needed (this is the same as multiplying 7.81 by 1,000, or 10^3).

$$\begin{array}{cc} \text{power of 10} & \text{add a zero} \\ \downarrow & \downarrow \end{array}$$
$$7.81 \times 10^3 = 7.8\,1\,0 = 7,810.0$$
$$\rightarrow\rightarrow\rightarrow$$

Answer: The number 7.81×10^3 written in standard form is 7,810.

Example 2: Write 27,651 in scientific notation.

Place a decimal point after the first digit to change 27,651 to a decimal number, which then must be multiplied by 10 raised to a power. To find the power of 10, count the number of digits after the decimal. The number of digits is the power of 10.

$$\begin{array}{cc} \text{add a decimal point} & \text{power of 10} \\ \downarrow & \downarrow \end{array}$$
$$27,651 = 2 \,.\, \underset{\text{4 digits}}{\underline{7\,6\,5\,1}} \times 10^4$$

Answer: The number 27,651 written in scientific notation is 2.7651×10^4.

Order of Operations

When we use a combination of addition, subtraction, multiplication, and division to solve problems, we must follow the **order of operations**: parentheses, exponents, multiplication, division, addition, subtraction. The acronym **PEMDAS** can help us remember the order.

Parentheses	Exponent	Multiply	Divide	Add	Subtract
P	E	M	D	A	S

Example: Evaluate: $36 \div (5 - 1) + 3^2$

$36 \div (5 - 1) + 3^2 \rightarrow$ 1. Evaluate the expression inside the parentheses (*P*).

$\downarrow$

$36 \div 4 + 3^2 \rightarrow$ 2. Evaluate the exponent (*E*).

$\downarrow$

$36 \div 4 + 9 \rightarrow$ 3. There is no multiplication (*M*); proceed to division (*D*).

$\downarrow$

$9 + 9 \rightarrow$ 4. Add (*A*). There is no subtraction (*S*).

$\downarrow$

18

Answer: $36 \div (5 - 1) + 3^2 = 18$

Factors

Factors are the numbers that are multiplied together to get a product. A number can have two or more factors.

Example 1: What are the factors of 18?

Find the numbers that make the equation $\Box \times \Box = 18$ true.

$$\boxed{1} \times \boxed{18} = 18 \qquad \boxed{2} \times \boxed{9} = 18 \qquad \boxed{3} \times \boxed{6} = 18$$

Answer: The factors of 18 are 1, 2, 3, 6, 9, and 18.

Example 2: What is the GCF of 12 and 16?

Find the numbers that make $\Box \times \Box = 12$ and $\Box \times \Box = 16$ true. Circle the common factors. The **greatest common factor** (GCF) is the common factor that has the largest value.

Factors of 12: ① ② 3 ④ 6 12

Factors of 16: ① ② ④ 8 16

Answer: The greatest common factor (GCF) of 12 and 16 is 4.

Multiples

The **multiples** of a given number are the products of that number and any other whole number.

Example 1: What are the first four multiples of 2?

Multiply 2 by 1, 2, 3, and 4.

multiple of 2 ↓

$$2 \times 1 = \boxed{2} \qquad 2 \times 2 = \boxed{4} \qquad 2 \times 3 = \boxed{6} \qquad 2 \times 4 = \boxed{8}$$

Answer: The first four multiples of 2 are 2, 4, 6, and 8.

Example 2: What is the least common multiple (LCM) of 6 and 8?

The **least common multiple** (LCM) is the first common multiple that a set of numbers share. Find the first few multiples of 6 and 8. Write (...) to show that there are many more multiples possible. Circle the first multiple that 6 and 8 have in common.

Multiples of 6: 6 12 18 ㉔ ...

Multiples of 8: 8 16 ㉔ 32 ...

Answer: The least common multiple (LCM) of 6 and 8 is 24.

We will use the GCF to simplify fractions. We will use the LCM when we add and subtract fractions.

Fractions and Mixed Numbers

A **fraction** represents part of a whole or part of a set. The bottom number is called the **denominator** and represents the number of equal parts in a whole (halves, fourths, etc.), or the total number of objects in a set. The top number is called the **numerator** and represents the parts that we are interested in.

$$\frac{1}{2} \begin{array}{l} \leftarrow \text{numerator} \\ \leftarrow \text{denominator} \end{array}$$

A **mixed number** is made up of a whole number and a fraction. When we read a mixed number, we say the whole number, the word *and*, and then the fraction.

Example 1: What fraction does the diagram represent?

The whole is divided into three equal parts, so the denominator is 3. There are two parts shaded, so the numerator is 2.

Answer: $\frac{2}{3}$

Example 2: What mixed number does the diagram represent?

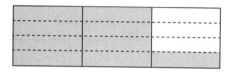

There are two wholes that are completely shaded, so the whole number is 2. There is one whole that is divided into four equal parts with one part shaded, so the denominator of the fraction is 4 and the numerator is 1.

Answer: $2\frac{1}{4}$ or two and one-fourth

Improper Fractions

A mixed number can be written as an **improper fraction**. In an improper fraction, the numerator is always larger than the denominator.

Imagine that $2\frac{1}{4}$ in the previous example represents two whole cups of sugar plus an additional part of a cup. How many *total parts* are there? The denominator in the fraction tells us that 1 whole cup is divided into fourths, or four parts. So, two whole cups equals eight parts. Those eight parts plus the remaining part give us nine parts. That is, we have $\frac{1}{4}$ cup of sugar, nine times. So, $2\frac{1}{4}$ as an improper fraction is $\frac{9}{4}$,

or nine fourths. This is NOT the same as $9\frac{1}{4}$, which is nine and one-fourth.

Example 1: Write $5\frac{1}{2}$ as an improper fraction.

To find the numerator of the improper fraction, multiply the denominator and the whole number, and then add the numerator. The denominator stays the same. Remember, we are finding how many parts we have in total, and the denominator tells us exactly what that part is.

$$\text{whole number} \rightarrow 5\frac{1}{2} = \frac{(2 \times 5) + 1}{2} = \frac{10 + 1}{2} = \frac{11}{2}$$

with "numerator" labeling the 1 and "denominator" labeling the 2.

Answer: $5\frac{1}{2} = \frac{11}{2}$ or eleven halves

$5\frac{1}{2}$ is equal to $\frac{1}{2}$, 11 times.

Example 2: Write $\frac{7}{4}$ as a mixed number.

We are finding out how many fourths go into 7. Rewrite the improper fraction as a division problem.

$$\frac{7}{4} = 7 \div 4 = 4\overline{)7}$$

Use the whole number part of the quotient as the whole number part of the mixed number. Use the remainder as the numerator of the fraction. The denominator stays the same. Here we have 1 whole and 3 parts left.

$$\text{denominator} \rightarrow 4\overline{)7} \quad \begin{array}{r} 1 \leftarrow \text{whole number} \\ \underline{-4} \\ 3 \leftarrow \text{numerator} \end{array}$$

Answer: $\frac{7}{4} = 1\frac{3}{4}$, or one and three fourths

$\frac{7}{4}$ is 1 whole ($\frac{1}{4}$, 4 times) and 3 parts ($\frac{1}{4}$, 3 times).

Simplifying Fractions

When we simplify a fraction, we *rename* the fraction to get the smallest numerator and denominator possible. We use the GCF of the numerator and the denominator to simplify a fraction to its lowest terms.

Example: Simplify: $\frac{2}{6}$

Find the GCF of 2 and 6. Divide the numerator and the denominator by the GCF.

$$\overset{\text{GCF}}{\underset{\downarrow}{}}$$
$$\frac{2 \div 2}{6 \div 2} = \frac{1}{3}$$

Answer: $\frac{2}{6} = \frac{1}{3}$

Adding and Subtracting Fractions and Mixed Numbers

Visualize pouring $\frac{1}{6}$ cup of sugar into $\frac{1}{4}$ cup of sugar.

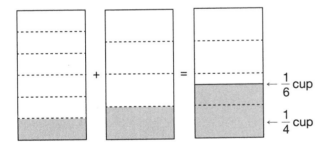

$\leftarrow \frac{1}{6}$ cup

$\leftarrow \frac{1}{4}$ cup

When the denominators are different, it is difficult to express the number of equal parts in the sum. To add and subtract fractions, the denominators must be the same.

Example 1: Add: $\frac{1}{6} + \frac{1}{4}$

The denominators are different, so find the LCM of the denominators. The least common multiple of the denominators is called the **least common denominator** (LCD).

Multiples of 4: 4 8 ⑫ 16 . . .

Multiples of 6: 6 ⑫ 18 24 . . .

Rename $\frac{1}{6}$ by multiplying the denominator by 2 to get the LCD of 12. Multiply the numerator by the same factor. Rename $\frac{1}{4}$ by multiplying the denominator by 3 to get the LCD of 12. Multiply the numerator by the same factor.

$$\frac{1 \times 2}{6 \times 2} = \frac{2}{12} \qquad \frac{1 \times 3}{4 \times 3} = \frac{3}{12}$$

We can now see how many twelfths we have. Add the numerators of the renamed fractions. Do NOT add the denominators.

$$\frac{2}{12} + \frac{3}{12} = \frac{2+3}{12} = \frac{5}{12}$$

Answer: $\frac{1}{6} + \frac{1}{4} = \frac{5}{12}$

Example 2: Subtract: $5\frac{1}{2} - 1\frac{1}{3}$

Line up the whole numbers and the decimals.

$$5\frac{1}{2}$$
$$-\ 1\frac{1}{3}$$

Rename the fractions using the least common denominator (LCD), or the least common multiple of 2 and 3 (which is 6).

$$5\frac{1 \times 3}{2 \times 3} = 5\frac{3}{6}$$
$$1\frac{1 \times 2}{3 \times 2} = 1\frac{2}{6}$$

We can now see how many sixths we have. Subtract the numerators of the fractions. Do NOT subtract the denominators. Then subtract the whole numbers.

$$5\frac{3}{6}$$
$$-1\frac{2}{6}$$
$$5 - 1 \rightarrow 4\frac{1}{6} \begin{matrix} \leftarrow 3-2 \\ \leftarrow \text{stays the same} \end{matrix}$$

Answer: $5\frac{1}{2} - 1\frac{1}{3} = 4\frac{1}{6}$

Multiplying and Dividing Fractions and Mixed Numbers

We can multiply and divide fractions and mixed numbers with like and unlike denominators. We do not need to rename the fractions with unlike denominators, but we need to convert mixed numbers to improper fractions.

Example 1: Multiply: $2\frac{1}{4} \times 1\frac{2}{3}$

Convert the mixed numbers to improper fractions. Multiply the numerators and then multiply the denominators.

$$2\frac{1}{4} \times 1\frac{2}{3} = \frac{9 \times 5}{4 \times 3} = \frac{45}{12}$$

Simplify the improper fraction using the greatest common factor (GCF) of 12 and 45.

$$\begin{array}{c} \text{GCF} \\ \downarrow \\ \frac{45 \div 3}{12 \div 3} = \frac{15}{4} \end{array}$$

Divide to convert the improper fraction back into a mixed number.

$$\begin{array}{r} 3 \leftarrow \text{whole number} \\ \text{denominator} \rightarrow 4\overline{)15} \\ \underline{-12} \\ 3 \leftarrow \text{numerator} \end{array}$$

Answer: $2\frac{1}{4} \times 1\frac{2}{3} = 3\frac{3}{4}$

Example 2: Divide: $\frac{3}{8} \div \frac{1}{3}$

Change the second fraction into its reciprocal (simply invert the numerator and denominator) and the division sign into a multiplication sign.

$$\begin{array}{c} \text{reciprocal of } \frac{1}{3} \\ \downarrow \\ \frac{3}{8} \div \frac{1}{3} = \frac{3}{8} \times \frac{3}{1} \end{array}$$

Multiply the numerators. Then multiply the denominators.

$$\frac{3 \times 3}{8 \times 1} = \frac{9}{8}$$

Divide to convert the improper fraction into a mixed number.

$$\begin{array}{r} 1 \leftarrow \text{whole number} \\ \text{denominator} \rightarrow 8\overline{)9} \\ \underline{-8} \\ 1 \leftarrow \text{numerator} \end{array}$$

Answer: $\frac{3}{8} \div \frac{1}{3} = 1\frac{1}{8}$

Comparing and Ordering Fractions and Mixed Numbers

To compare and order fractions, rename the fractions using the LCD. Then compare the numerators of the renamed fractions.

Example: Order $\frac{1}{6}, \frac{2}{3}, \frac{1}{2}$, and $\frac{4}{5}$ from least to greatest.

Rename the fractions using the LCD of 2, 3, 5, and 6 (which is 30).

$$\frac{1 \times 5}{6 \times 5} = \frac{5}{30} \qquad \frac{2 \times 10}{3 \times 10} = \frac{20}{30} \qquad \frac{1 \times 15}{2 \times 15} = \frac{15}{30} \qquad \frac{4 \times 6}{5 \times 6} = \frac{24}{30}$$

Order the renamed fractions from least to greatest by ordering the numerators.

$$\frac{5}{30}, \frac{15}{30}, \frac{20}{30}, \frac{24}{30}$$

Answer: The order of the fractions from least to greatest is $\frac{1}{6}, \frac{1}{2}, \frac{2}{3}, \frac{4}{5}$.

Fractions, Decimals, and Percentages

Fractions, decimals, and percentages all represent parts of a whole. If we have a set of 100 coins and 75 of those coins are pennies, we can express 75 out of

100 as $\frac{75}{100}$, 0.75, or 75%. We use division and powers of 10 to convert between fractions, decimals, and percentages.

Example 1:
A. Write $\frac{3}{5}$ as a decimal.

Rewrite the fraction as a division problem. Think: $5 \times \boxed{?}$ is less than or equal to 3. Multiply and then subtract.

$$\begin{array}{r} \boxed{0} \\ 5\overline{)3} \\ \underline{-0} \\ 3 \end{array}$$

The number 3 is the same as 3.0. Add a 0 in the first decimal place and then bring down the 0. Think: $5 \times \boxed{?}$ is less than or equal to 30. Multiply and then subtract.

$$\begin{array}{r} 0\,\boxed{6} \\ 5\overline{)3.0} \\ \underline{-0}\downarrow \\ 3\;0 \\ \underline{-3\;0} \\ 0 \end{array}$$

Line up the decimal point in the answer with the decimal point in 3.0.

$$\begin{array}{r} 0.6 \\ 5\overline{)3.0} \end{array}$$

Answer: $\frac{3}{5} = 0.6$

B. Write $\frac{3}{5}$ as a percent.

A **percent** is a fraction with a denominator of 100. To rename $\frac{3}{5}$ as a fraction with a denominator of 100,

multiply the denominator and the numerator by 20. Write the percent using the numerator of the renamed fraction and the percent sign (%).

$$\frac{3 \times 20}{5 \times 20} = \frac{60}{100} = 60\%$$

Answer: $\frac{3}{5} = 0.6 = 60\%$

Example 2:
A. Write 0.25 as a fraction.

Write the digits of the decimal as the numerator of the fraction. Count the number of decimal places in 0.25. The number of decimal places tells us the power of 10 to use for the denominator of the fraction. There are 2 decimal places in 0.25, so the denominator is 10^2 or 100.

$$\begin{array}{c} \text{2 decimal places} \\ \downarrow \\ 0.25 = \frac{25}{10^2} = \frac{25}{100} \end{array}$$

Simplify the fraction using the greatest common factor (GCF) of 25 and 100.

$$\begin{array}{c} \text{GCF} \\ \downarrow \\ \frac{25 \div 25}{100 \div 25} = \frac{1}{4} \end{array}$$

Answer: $0.25 = \frac{1}{4}$

B. Write 0.25 as a percent.

Write 0.25 as a fraction with a numerator of 25 and a denominator of 100, like in Example 2-A. Write the percentage equivalent using the numerator and the percent sign (%).

$$0.25 = \frac{25}{100} = 25\%$$

Answer: $0.25 = 25\%$

Example 3:
A. Write 8% as a fraction.

The number in front of the percent sign is the numerator of the fraction. The denominator is always 100.

$$8\% = \frac{8}{100}$$

Simplify the fraction using the greatest common factor (GCF) of 8 and 100 (which is 4).

$$\frac{8 \div 4}{100 \div 4} = \frac{2}{25}$$

Answer: $8\% = \frac{2}{25}$

B. Write 8% as a decimal.

Write 8% as a fraction with a denominator of 100. We can follow a special pattern to find the decimal equivalent. Since there are two 0s in 100, we move the decimal point in the numerator two places to the left.

$$\frac{8}{100} = \frac{8.0}{100} = 0.\underset{\leftarrow\leftarrow}{0\,8}$$

We can follow this pattern when the denominator is 10, 100, 1000, and so on.

$$\frac{8}{10} = \frac{8.0}{10} = 0.\underset{\leftarrow}{8} \qquad \frac{8}{1,000} = \frac{8.0}{1,000} = 0.\underset{\leftarrow\leftarrow\leftarrow}{0\,0\,8}$$

Answer: $8\% = 0.08$

Comparing and Ordering Fractions, Decimals, and Percentages

To compare and order fractions, decimals, and percentages, convert the fractions and percentages to their decimal equivalents.

Example: Order 37%, $\frac{1}{2}$, and 2.9 from greatest to least.

Convert the percent and the fraction to their decimal equivalents.

$$37\% = \frac{37}{100} = 0.37 \text{ and } \frac{1}{2} = 0.5$$

Line up the decimal points and the digits by their place value. Compare the digits, one place value at a time. Since 2 ones is greater than 0 ones, 2.9 is greater than 0.37 and 0.5. Since 5 tenths is greater than 3 tenths, 0.5 is greater than 0.37.

$$5 \text{ tenths} > 3 \text{ tenths}$$
$$\downarrow$$
$$0.37$$
$$0.50$$
$$2 \text{ ones} > 0 \text{ ones} \rightarrow 2.90$$

Answer: The order from greatest to least is 2.9, $\frac{1}{2}$, and 37%.

Percent Problems

We can solve percent problems using the **percent equation** or the **percent triangle**.

Percent Equation	Percent Triangle
part = percent × whole	

Example 1: What is 32% of 8? Use the percent equation.

The word "is" represents the equals sign, and the word "of" represents the multiplication sign in the percent equation. The number 8 represents the whole. Express 32% as a decimal and multiply by 8 to find the part.

what   is   32%   of   8
↓   ↓   ↓   ↓   ↓

part = percent × whole

$\boxed{?} = 0.32 \times 8$

$\boxed{?} = 2.56$

Answer: 32% of 8 is 2.56

Example 2: 6 is what percent of 12? Use the percent triangle.

Fill in the percent triangle with the given numbers. The division sign between the two numbers tells us to divide.

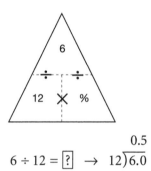

$6 \div 12 = \boxed{?} \quad \rightarrow \quad 12\overline{)6.0}^{\,0.5}$

Convert the decimal to a fraction with a denominator of 100. Then convert the fraction to a percent.

$$0.5 = \frac{5 \times 10}{10 \times 10} = \frac{50}{100} = 50\%$$

Answer: 6 is 50% of 12

Ratios and Proportions

A **ratio** compares two numbers. It can be written as a fraction in simplest terms, with the word "to," or with a colon. A **proportion** is an equation that shows two equivalent ratios.

Example 1:

A. What is the ratio of squares to triangles?

The diagram shows 3 squares and 6 triangles. Write the ratio as a fraction with the number of squares as the numerator. Simplify the fraction.

$$\frac{\text{squares}}{\text{triangles}} = \frac{3}{6} = \frac{1}{2}$$

Answer: The ratio of squares to triangles is $\frac{1}{2}$. The ratio can also be written as "1 to 2" or 1:2.

It is important to pay attention to the order of the numbers in a ratio. The ratio 1:2 tells us that for every 1 square, there are 2 triangles. The ratio 1:2 does not represent the ratio of triangles to squares.

B. What is the ratio of triangles to squares?

Write the ratio as a fraction with the number of triangles as the numerator. Simplify the fraction.

$$\frac{\text{triangles}}{\text{squares}} = \frac{6}{3} = \frac{2}{1}$$

Answer: The ratio of triangles to squares is $\frac{2}{1}$ or "2 to 1" or 2:1.

Example 2: Are the ratios $\frac{3}{4}$ and $\frac{10}{16}$ proportional?

Cross multiply the ratios. To **cross multiply** means to multiply the numerator of one ratio by the denominator of the other ratio.

Cross product 1 is the product of the numerator of the first ratio and the denominator of the second ratio. Cross product 2 is the product of the numerator of the second ratio and the denominator of the first ratio. If the cross products are equal, then the ratios form a proportion. If the cross products are not equal, the ratios do not form a proportion.

cross product 1   cross product 2

$$\downarrow \qquad ? \qquad \downarrow$$
$$3 \times 16 \quad = \quad 10 \times 4$$
$$48 \quad \neq \quad 40$$

Answer: The ratios $\frac{3}{4}$ and $\frac{10}{16}$ are not proportional.

TIP

A quick and easy way to remember the products of 9×2 to 9×9 is to hold out both of your hands with your fingers extended and palms facing down. If you are multiplying 9 by 4, fold down the fourth finger from the left, which is the finger next to the thumb on your left hand. Count the number of fingers to the left of the one you folded to represent the number in the tens place (3). Then count the number of fingers to its right to represent the number in the ones place (6). When you put the numbers together, you should have the number 36. So, $9 \times 4 = 36$.

Quiz

1. What is the value of the 9 in 4702.9?
   a. 9 thousandths
   b. 9 hundredths
   c. 9 tenths
   d. 9 ones
   e. 9 tens

2. Which choice has 872.5, 93.7, and 2.740 in correct order from greatest to least?
   a. 872.5, 93.7, and 2.740
   b. 2.740, 872.5, and 93.7
   c. 93.7, 872.5, and 2.740
   d. 2.740, 93.7, and 872.5
   e. 872.5, 2.740, and 93.7

3. Round 3.574 to the nearest hundredth.
   a. 3.000
   b. 3.500
   c. 3.570
   d. 3.580
   e. 3.600

4. What is the sum of $0.837 + 0.291$?
   a. 0.1128
   b. 1.128
   c. 11.28
   d. 112.8
   e. 1,128

5. Determine the product of 3×6^2.
   a. 15
   b. 36
   c. 64
   d. 100
   e. 108

6. Which of the following is 2.43×10^4 in standard form?

a. 243

b. 2,430

c. 24,300

d. 243,000

e. 2,430,000

7. What is the least common multiple (LCM) of 3 and 12?

a. 3

b. 6

c. 9

d. 12

e. 36

8. Subtract: $3\frac{5}{6} - 1\frac{2}{3}$. Simplify the fraction to its lowest terms.

a. $2\frac{1}{2}$

b. $2\frac{1}{6}$

c. $2\frac{1}{4}$

d. $2\frac{2}{3}$

e. $2\frac{3}{4}$

9. Which of the following has 0.67, $\frac{3}{4}$, and 10% in order from least to greatest?

a. 10%, 0.67, $\frac{3}{4}$

b. 0.67, $\frac{3}{4}$, 10%

c. $\frac{3}{4}$, 10%, 0.67

d. 0.67, 10%, $\frac{3}{4}$

e. 10%, $\frac{3}{4}$, 0.67

10. What is the ratio of the number of weekdays to the number of weekend days in one week? Write your ratio as a fraction.

Quiz Answers

1. c. The number 9 is to the right of the decimal point, which means it will be an answer with "-ths" attached to it. Therefore, choices **d** and **e** can be eliminated. Since 9 is the first number to the right of the decimal, it is in the tenths place, so its value is 9 tenths.

2. a. The key here is to align the numbers so that the decimals are all even with one another.

8　7　2.5

|0|　9　3.7

|0||0|　2.740

Done this way, even though 872.5 and 2.740 have 4 digits each, the placement of the decimal makes it apparent that 872.5 is the largest number because it is the only one to have a hundreds digit. 93.7 is the second largest because it has a tens digit, and 2.740 does not, so it is the smallest.

3. c. The 7 is in the hundredths place, and it is followed by a 4. Recalling the Tip Box that noted "Four or less, let it rest," the number should remain a 7, not be rounded up to 8. This makes the final rounding 3.570.

4. b. Again, correct alignment of the two numbers is the initial step required to get a correct answer.

0.837

0.291

After this step, proper regrouping must occur. 7 + 1 is 8, but 3 + 9 = 12, so the 2 is written down and the 1 is carried over. That makes the tenths column 1 + 8 + 2, which equals 11. Again, regrouping occurs, and a 1 is left in the tenths column while the "ten tenths" is placed in the ones column to the left of the decimal. This gives you 1.128.

```
        1  1         0+1 ones    +1 tenth
  0.837 →    0 ones  . 8 tenths  3 hundredths  7 thousandths
 +0.291 →   −0 ones  . 2 tenths  9 hundredths  1 thousandths
  1.128       1 ones . 1 tenths  2 hundredths  8 thousandths
```

5. e. The exponent 2 above 6 means *six squared* or (6×6), not (6×2) as sometimes thought. $(6 \times 6) = 36$, so the question asks, *what is 3×36*? The answer is 108.

Note that if you multiplied 3 and 6 first before dealing with the exponent, you would have been making an order of operations error.

6. c. The key to scientific notation is taking the exponent attached to the 10 and then moving the decimal point the proper number of spaces in one direction or the other, adding zeros where needed. Since the exponent 4 is positive, the decimal is moved 4 spaces to the right. (If the exponent were negative, the decimal would be moved to the left.) This results in a standard form of 24,300.

7. d. 3 is a factor of 12, since $3 \times 4 = 12$, so 12 is the least common multiple of 3 and 12.

8. b. First, change the fractions so that they have the same denominator.

$$3\frac{5 \times 1}{6 \times 1} = 3\frac{5}{6}$$

$$1\frac{2 \times 2}{3 \times 2} = 1\frac{4}{6}$$

$5 - 4$ is 1, and so the fraction is $\frac{1}{6}$. $3 - 1$ is 2, so the whole number is 2. Therefore, the mixed number is $2\frac{1}{6}$.

9. a. For this question, all values should be converted to one form. This explanation will use percentages, but fractions or decimals could just as easily be used. 10% remains the same. For 0.67, the decimal point moves two places to the right and it becomes 67%. For $\frac{3}{4}$, the denominator and numerator must both be multiplied by a number that changes the denominator to 100. For this fraction, that number is 25.

$$\frac{3}{4} \times \frac{25}{25} = \frac{75}{100} = 75\%$$

This makes the correct order (least to greatest) 10%, 0.67, $\frac{3}{4}$.

10. **Answer:** See Grid

There are 5 weekdays and 2 weekends in one week, so the ratio is $\frac{5}{2}$.

Whole Numbers and Decimals

We use place value to read, round, and compare whole numbers and decimals. We also use place value and regrouping to add, subtract, multiply, and divide. When we use a combination of addition, subtraction, multiplication, and division to solve problems, we must remember to follow the order of operations.

Fractions and Mixed Numbers

We use the greatest common factor and the least common multiple when we solve problems involving fractions and mixed numbers. When we add and subtract fractions, we need to rename the fractions so that they have the same denominator. We rename them by using the least common multiple of their denominators. When we simplify fractions, we use the greatest common factor of the numerator and the denominator.

Fractions, Decimals, and Percentages

We use division and powers of 10 to convert between fractions, decimals, and percentages. Remember that a percent is a fraction with a denominator of 100. Use the percent equation or the percent triangle to solve percent problems.

Ratios and Proportions

A ratio compares two numbers. It is important to pay attention to the order of the numbers. A ratio can be written as a fraction, with the word "to," or with a colon. A proportion is an equation that shows two equivalent ratios.

 GEOMETRY AND MEASUREMENT

CHAPTER SUMMARY
In this chapter, you will learn about units of measurement, number lines, the coordinate plane, angles, polygons, circles, and solids.

Geometry is the study of shapes and the relationships among them. The geometry that you are required to know for the GED® Math test is fundamental and practical. You should get familiar with the properties of angles, lines, polygons, triangles, and circles, as well as with the formulas for area, volume, and perimeter. A grasp of coordinate geometry will also be important when you take the GED® Test.

Units of Measurement

The **customary system** and the **metric system** are the two systems of measurement used to measure length, weight/mass, and capacity.

Customary System of Measurement

The following table lists the most commonly used customary units of length, weight, and capacity. For each type of measurement, the units are listed in order from smallest to largest. For example, the inch is smaller than the foot, the foot is smaller than the yard, and the yard is smaller than the mile.

Customary Units of Length	Customary Units of Weight	Customary Units of Capacity
inch (in.)	ounce (oz.)	fluid ounce (fl. oz.)
foot (ft.)	pound (lb.)	cup (c.)
yard (yd.)	ton (T)	pint (pt.)
mile (mi.)		quart (qt.)
		gallon (gal.)

We can convert from one unit to another by either multiplying or dividing by a conversion factor. We multiply to convert from a larger unit to a smaller unit. We divide to convert from a smaller unit to a larger unit.

		Converting from larger → smaller		Converting from smaller → larger	
		To convert	multiply by	To convert	divide by
Length					
	1 ft. = 12 in.	ft. → in.	12	in. → ft.	12
	1 yd. = 3 ft.	yd. → ft	3	ft. → yd.	3
	1 mi. = 1,760 yd.	mi. → yd.	1,760	yd. → mi.	1,760
Weight					
	1 lb. = 16 oz.	lb. → oz.	16	oz. → lb.	16
	1 T = 2,000 lb.	T → lb.	2,000	lb. → T	2,000
Capacity					
	1 c. = 8 fl. oz.	c. → fl oz.	8	fl oz. → c.	8
	1 pt. = 2c.	pt. → c.	2	c. → pt.	2
	1 qt. = 2 pt.	qt. → pt.	2	pt. → qt.	2
	1 gal. = 4 qt.	gal. → qt.	4	qt. → gal.	4

Example 1: Solve: 6 ft. = $\boxed{?}$ in.

To convert from feet (larger unit) to inches (smaller unit), we multiply the number of feet by 12 because there are 12 inches in one foot:

$$6 \times 12 = 72$$

Answer: 6 ft. = 72 in.

Example 2: Solve: 48 oz. = $\boxed{?}$ lb.

To convert from ounces (smaller unit) to pounds (larger unit), we divide the number of ounces by 16 because there are 16 ounces in one pound:

$$48 \div 16 = 3$$

Answer: 48 oz. = 3 lb.

Metric System of Measurement

The following table lists the most commonly used metric units of length, mass, and capacity.

Metric Units of Length	Metric Units of Weight	Metric Units of Capacity
millimeter (mm)	milligram (mg)	milliliter (mL)
centimeter (cm)	gram (g)	liter (L)
meter (m)	kilogram (kg)	
kilometer (km)		

As with the customary system of measurement, we either multiply or divide to convert from one unit to another. However, with the metric system of measurement, we multiply or divide by a power of 10.

	Converting from larger → smaller		Converting from smaller → larger	
	To convert	**multiply by**	**To convert**	**divide by**
Length				
1 cm = 10 mm	cm → mm	10 or 10^1	mm → cm	10 or 10^1
1 m = 100 cm	m → cm	100 or 10^2	cm → m	100 or 10^2
1 km = 1,000 m	km → m	1,000 or 10^3	m → km	1,000 or 10^3
Mass				
1 g = 1,000 mg	g → mg	1,000 or 10^3	mg → g	1,000 or 10^3
1 kg = 1,000 g	kg → g	1,000 or 10^3	g → kg	1,000 or 10^3
Capacity				
1 L = 1,000 mL	L → mL	1,000 or 10^3	mL → L	1,000 or 10^3

Recall from Chapter 1 that when we multiply by a power of 10, we simply move the decimal point to the right and add zeros as needed. Similarly, when we divide by a power of 10, we move the decimal point to the left.

Example 1: Solve: 14 kg = $\boxed{?}$ g

To convert from kilograms (larger unit) to grams (smaller unit), we multiply the number of kilograms by 1,000 (or move the decimal point 3 places to the right) because there are 1,000 grams in one kilogram.

$$14 \times 1,000 = 14.0 \times 10^3 = 14\ 0\ 0\ 0 = 14,000$$
$$\rightarrow \rightarrow \rightarrow$$

Answer: 14 kg = 14,000 g

Example 2: Solve: 75 cm = $\boxed{?}$ m

To convert from centimeters (smaller unit) to meters (larger unit), we divide by 100 (or move the decimal point 2 places to the left) because there are 100 centimeters in one meter.

$$75 \div 100 = \frac{75.0}{100} = 0.\,7\,5$$
$$\leftarrow \leftarrow$$

Answer: 75 cm = 0.75 m

TIP

The metric system uses the same set of prefixes for units of length, mass, and capacity: milli-, centi-, and kilo- (for example, millimeter, milligram, and milliliter). To help you remember the prefixes in order from smallest to largest (milli-, centi-, kilo-), use the following mnemonic (or make up your own!).

Mary **C**atches **K**angaroos

Number Lines

A **line** is made up of an infinite set of **points** extending in opposite directions. A **number line** is a line in which numbers are assigned to those points.

Notice that the numbers to the left of 0 have a negative (–) sign. These numbers are called **negative numbers**. The numbers to the right of 0 are called **positive numbers**. Positive numbers can be written with or without a positive (+) sign.

Positive and negative numbers are opposites of each other. For example, 4 and –4 are opposites.

Finding Points on a Number Line
Example:

A. Which point represents $\frac{3}{4}$?

Since $\frac{3}{4}$ is greater than 0 and less than 1, the point that represents $\frac{3}{4}$ lies between 0 and 1.

Answer: Point C represents $\frac{3}{4}$.

B. Which point represents –2.5?

Think: +2.5 is between +2 and +3, so –2.5 is between –2 and –3.

Answer: Point B represents –2.5.

Adding Positive and Negative Numbers
Number lines can help us add positive and negative numbers. We can visualize adding a positive number as moving to the right on the number line. We can visualize adding a negative number as moving to the left.

Example 1: Add: 5 + (−2)

Start at 5. To add −2, move 2 units to the left.

Answer: 5 + (−2) = 3

Example 2: Add: −8 + 10

Start at −8. To add 10, move 10 units to the right.

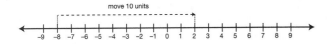

Answer: −8 + 10 = 2

Subtracting Positive and Negative Numbers

To subtract a positive or negative number, we *add* its *opposite*.

Example 1: Subtract: −5 − 1

The opposite of 1 is −1, so we rewrite −5 − 1 as −5 + (−1).

Answer: −5 − 1 = − 6

Example 2: Subtract: −7 − (−7)

The opposite of −7 is 7, so we rewrite −7 − (−7) as −7 + 7.

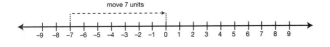

Answer: −7 − (−7) = 0

Multiplying and Dividing Positive and Negative Numbers

We multiply and divide positive and negative numbers the same way we multiply and divide whole numbers. However, the answer is either positive or negative depending on the signs of the factors.

If the two factors are both positive or both negative, the answer is positive.

$$(+) \times (+) = (+) \qquad (+) \div (+) = (+)$$
$$(-) \times (-) = (+) \qquad (-) \div (-) = (+)$$

If one factor is positive and the other is negative, the answer is negative.

$$(+) \times (-) = (-) \qquad (+) \div (-) = (-)$$
$$(-) \times (+) = (-) \qquad (-) \div (+) = (-)$$

Example 1: Multiply: −11 × −9

Both factors are negative, so the answer is positive.

Answer: −11 × −9 = 99

Example 2: Divide: −24 ÷ 2

One factor is positive and the other is negative, so the answer is negative.

Answer: −24 ÷ 2 = −12

The Coordinate Plane

A **coordinate plane** is made up of a vertical and a horizontal number line. The horizontal number line is called the *x*-axis. The vertical number line is called the *y*-axis. The point of intersection of the axes is called **the origin** (*O*).

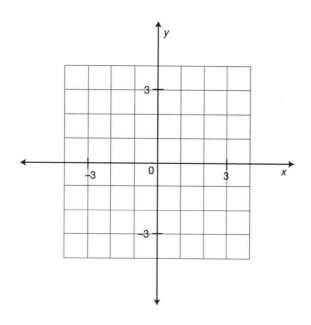

Numbers to the right of the origin are positive. Numbers to the left of the origin are negative. Similarly, numbers above the origin are positive. Numbers below the origin are negative.

Finding Points on a Coordinate Plane

Each point on a coordinate plane is represented by an **ordered pair** of numbers (x,y). For example, the coordinates of the origin are $(0,0)$. The first number comes from the x-axis and is called the **x-coordinate**. The second number comes from the y-axis and is called the **y-coordinate**.

If the x-coordinate is positive, we move to the right. If it is negative, we move to the left. If the y-coordinate is positive, we move up. If it is negative, we move down.

Example:

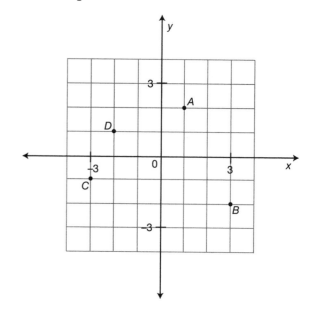

A. Which point is located at $(3,-2)$?

The ordered pair $(3,-2)$ tells us that the x-coordinate is 3 and the y-coordinate is -2. Starting from the origin (O), we move 3 units to the right. Then we move 2 units down.

Answer: Point B is located at $(3,-2)$.

B. What are the coordinates of Point D?

To reach point D, we move 2 units to the left from the origin. Then we move 1 unit up.

Answer: The coordinates of Point D are $(-2,1)$.

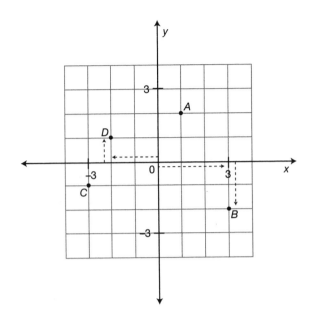

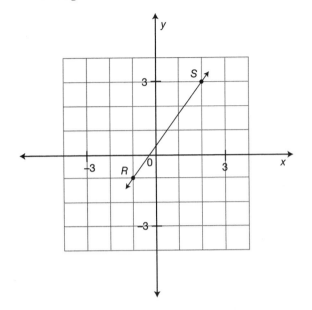

Example:

Distance between Two Points

Given two points (x_1, y_1) and (x_2, y_2) on a coordinate plane, we can find the distance between these points using the **distance formula**:

$$\text{distance between points} = \sqrt{(x_2 - x_1)^2 + (y_2 - y_1)^2}$$

Slope of a Line

Given two points (x_1, y_1) and (x_2, y_2), we can draw a straight line that passes through these points. The **slope** (m) is a measure of how steep that line is. The formula for finding the slope of a line is $m = \frac{y_2 - y_1}{x_2 - x_1}$.

A. What is the distance between Point R and Point S?

Point R is located at $(-1, -1)$, so $(x_1, y_1) = (-1, -1)$.
Point S is located at $(2, 3)$, so $(x_2, y_2) = (2, 3)$.

Plug the coordinates into the distance formula.

$$
\begin{aligned}
\text{distance between points} &= \sqrt{(x_2 - x_1)^2 + (y_2 - y_1)^2} \\
&= \sqrt{(2 - (-1))^2 + (3 - (-1))^2} \\
&= \sqrt{(2 + 1)^2 + (3 + 1)^2} \\
&= \sqrt{3^2 + 4^2} \\
&= \sqrt{9 + 16} \\
&= \sqrt{25} \\
&= 5
\end{aligned}
$$

Answer: The distance between Point R and Point S is 5 units.

B. What is the slope of the line that passes through Point R and Point S?

Plug the coordinates of Points R and S into the slope formula.

$$m = \frac{y_2 - y_1}{x_2 - x_1}$$
$$= \frac{3 - (-1)}{2 - (-1)}$$
$$= \frac{3 + 1}{2 + 1}$$
$$= \frac{4}{3}$$

Answer: The slope of the line that passes through Point R and Point S is $\frac{4}{3}$.

Note: Another way to think of the slope is moving 4 units up and 3 units over to get to Point S from Point R.

Parallel and Perpendicular Lines

When two lines have the same slope, they are called **parallel** lines. Parallel lines will never intersect. If the slopes of two lines are negative reciprocals of each other, their product will be −1, and the lines are **perpendicular**. Perpendicular lines intersect at one point.

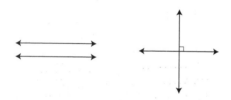

The square at the intersection of the perpendicular lines represents a right angle. We will learn more about right angles in the next section.

Example 1: Line a passes through the points $(1,2)$ and $(4,3)$. Line b passes through the points $(4,0)$ and $(1,-1)$. Are these lines parallel or perpendicular?

First, we find the slope of line a, using $(x_1,y_1) = (1,2)$ and $(x_2,y_2) = (4,3)$:

$$m = \frac{y_2 - y_1}{x_2 - x_1}$$
$$= \frac{3 - 2}{4 - 1}$$
$$= \frac{1}{3}$$

Then we find the slope of line b, using $(x_1,y_1) = (4,0)$ and $(x_2,y_2) = (1,-1)$:

$$m = \frac{y_2 - y_1}{x_2 - x_1}$$
$$= \frac{-1 - 0}{1 - 4}$$
$$= \frac{-1 - 0}{1 + (-4)}$$
$$= \frac{-1}{-3} \quad \leftarrow \text{remember, when dividing two negative numbers, the answer is positive}$$
$$= \frac{1}{3}$$

The two slopes are equal.

Answer: Line a and line b are parallel.

Example 2: Line a passes through the points $(0,0)$ and $(-2,2)$. Line b passes through $(-3,-1)$ and $(1,3)$. Are these lines parallel or perpendicular?

The slope of line a is

$$m = \frac{y_2 - y_1}{x_2 - x_1}$$
$$= \frac{2 - 0}{-2 - 0}$$
$$= \frac{2}{-2}$$
$$= -1$$

The slope of line b is

$$m = \frac{y_2 - y_1}{x_2 - x_1}$$

$$= \frac{3 - (-1)}{1 - (-3)}$$

$$= \frac{3 + 1}{1 + 3}$$

$$= \frac{4}{4}$$

$$= 1$$

The slopes are not equal, but the product of the two slopes is -1:

$$\underset{\downarrow}{\text{slope of line } a} \quad \underset{\downarrow}{\text{slope of line } b}$$

$$-1 \times 1 = -1$$

Answer: Line a and line b are perpendicular.

Angles

When two lines, or parts of lines, intersect, they form **angles**. Angles are measured in **degrees**. The symbol for *angle* is $\angle$ and the symbol for *degrees* is °.

An angle can be classified as **acute**, **right**, **obtuse**, or **straight**, depending on its measure.

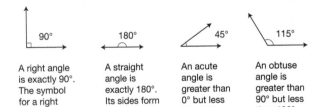

90°	180°	45°	115°
A right angle is exactly 90°. The symbol for a right angle is a square.	A straight angle is exactly 180°. Its sides form a straight line	An acute angle is greater than 0° but less than 90°.	An obtuse angle is greater than 90° but less than 180°.

Complementary and Supplementary Angles

If the sum of the measures of two angles is 90°, the angles are **complementary**. If the sum of the measures of two angles is 180°, the angles are **supplementary**.

Example 1: If $m\angle 1 = 40°$, what is $m\angle 2$?

$m\angle 1 = 40°$ tells us that the measure (m) of angle 1 is 40°. The square angle tells us that $\angle 1$ and $\angle 2$ are complementary angles, so the sum of their measures is 90°. To find the measure of $\angle 2$, we subtract.

$$m\angle 2 = 90° - m\angle 1$$

$$= 90° - 40°$$

$$= 50°$$

Answer: $m\angle 2 = 50°$

Example 2: If $m\angle 1 = 135°$, what is $m\angle 2$?

$\angle 1$ and $\angle 2$ are supplementary angles. Together they form a straight angle, so the sum of their measures is 180°. To find the measure of $\angle 2$, we subtract.

$$m\angle 2 = 180° - m\angle 1$$

$$= 180° - 135°$$

$$= 45°$$

Answer: $m\angle 2 = 45°$

Congruent Angles

The following diagram shows two parallel lines, *m* and *n*, cut by a third line called a **transversal**.

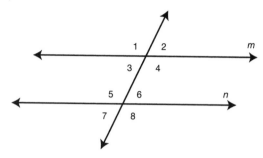

When parallel lines are cut by a transversal, they form **congruent** angles. Congruent means having the same measure. The symbol for congruent is ≅.

Vertical angles are congruent:

$\angle 1 \cong \angle 4$

$\angle 2 \cong \angle 3$

$\angle 5 \cong \angle 8$

$\angle 6 \cong \angle 7$

Corresponding angles are congruent:

$\angle 1 \cong \angle 5$

$\angle 2 \cong \angle 6$

$\angle 3 \cong \angle 7$

$\angle 4 \cong \angle 8$

Alternate interior angles are congruent:

$\angle 3 \cong \angle 6$

$\angle 4 \cong \angle 5$

Alternate exterior angles are congruent:

$\angle 1 \cong \angle 8$

$\angle 2 \cong \angle 7$

Example: Lines *m* and *n* are parallel lines cut by a transversal. $m\angle 1 = 120°$ and $m\angle 2 = 60°$.

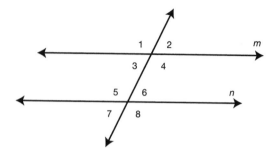

A. What is $m\angle 3$?

$\angle 2$ and $\angle 3$ are vertical angles, so $\angle 2 \cong \angle 3$

Answer: $m\angle 3 = 60°$

B. What is $m\angle 8$?

$\angle 1$ and $\angle 8$ are alternate exterior angles, so $\angle 1 \cong \angle 8$

Answer: $m\angle 8 = 120°$

Polygons

Polygons are two-dimensional figures with straight sides. Polygons with three sides are called **triangles** (*tri-* means "three"). Polygons with four sides are called **quadrilaterals** (*quad-* means "four"). Some common types of triangles and quadrilaterals are shown next. They are classified by their interior angles and by how many congruent (equal in length) and parallel sides they have, if any.

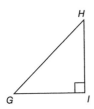

A right triangle has 1 right angle.

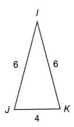

A scalene triangle has no congruent sides.

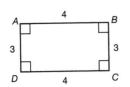

An isosceles triangle has at least 2 congruent sides.

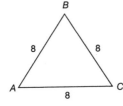

An equilateral triangle has 3 congruent sides.

A rectangle has 4 right angles. Opposite sides are parallel and congruent.

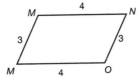

A trapezoid has exactly one pair of parallel sides.

A square has 4 congruent sides and 4 right angles. Opposite sides are parallel.

A parallelogram has opposite sides that are parallel and congruent.

Example: Classify the quadrilateral as a square, rectangle, parallelogram, or trapezoid.

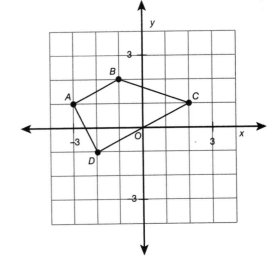

The vertices of quadrilateral *ABCD* are located at $A(-3,1)$, $B(-1,2)$, $C(2,1)$, $D(-2,-1)$. A **vertex** is the point where two sides of a polygon meet.

To classify the quadrilateral, we find the slopes of the sides to determine if there are any pairs that are parallel or perpendicular.

The slope of side *AB* is

$$m = \frac{y_2 - y_1}{x_2 - x_1}$$

$$= \frac{2 - 1}{-1 - (-3)}$$

$$= \frac{2 + (-1)}{-1 + 3}$$

$$= \frac{1}{2}$$

The slope of side *BC* is

$$m = \frac{y_2 - y_1}{x_2 - x_1}$$

$$= \frac{1 - 2}{2 - (-1)}$$

$$= \frac{1 + (-2)}{2 + 1}$$

$$= \frac{-1}{3}$$

The slope of side *CD* is

$$m = \frac{y_2 - y_1}{x_2 - x_1}$$

$$= \frac{-1 - 1}{-2 - 2}$$

$$= \frac{-1 + (-1)}{-2 + (-2)}$$

$$= \frac{-2}{-4}$$

$$= \frac{2}{4}$$

$$= \frac{1}{2}$$

The slope of side *AD* is

$$m = \frac{y_2 - y_1}{x_2 - x_1}$$

$$= \frac{-1 - 1}{-2 - (-3)}$$

$$= \frac{-1 + (-1)}{-2 + 3}$$

$$= \frac{-2}{1}$$

$$= -2$$

Quadrilateral *ABCD* has only one pair of parallel sides (side *AB* and side *CD*).

Answer: Quadrilateral *ABCD* is a trapezoid.

Angle Measures

The sum of the measures of the interior angles in any triangle is 180°. The sum of the measures of the interior angles in any quadrilateral is 360º.

Example 1: What is m∠B?

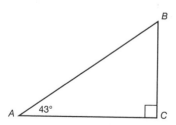

We know that the sum of all three interior angles in a triangle is 180°. We also know the measures of ∠A and ∠C. To find the measure of ∠B, we first find the sum of the measures of ∠A and ∠C.

$$m\angle A + m\angle C = 43° + 90° = 133°$$

Then we subtract that sum from the sum of all three angles.

$$m\angle B = 180° - 133° = 47°$$

Answer: $m\angle B = 47°$

Example 2: What is $m\angle H$?

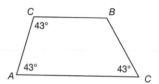

The sum of all four interior angles in a trapezoid is 360°. To find the measure of ∠H, we first find the sum of the measures of the other three angles.

$$m\angle G + m\angle I + m\angle J = 100° + 60° + 65° = 225°$$

Then we subtract that sum from the sum of all four angles.

$$m\angle H = 360° - 225° = 135°$$

Answer: $m\angle H = 135°$

Perimeter and Area

Perimeter refers to the total distance around a polygon. The formulas for finding the perimeter of triangles, squares, and rectangles are given next.

Triangle: Perimeter = $side_1 + side_2 + side_3$
Square: Perimeter = $4 \times side$
Rectangle: Perimeter = $2 \times length + 2 \times width$

Area refers to the space inside a polygon. The formulas for finding the area of triangles and quadrilaterals are given next.

Triangle: Area = $\frac{1}{2} \times base \times height$
Square: Area = $side^2$
Rectangle: Area = $length \times width$
Parallelogram: Area = $base \times height$
Trapezoid: Area = $\frac{1}{2} \times (base_1 + base_2)$
$\times height$

TIP

Many mathematical formulas are available to you when you take the real GED® Test, so while it is helpful to memorize the previous formulas, you do not need to do so. Be sure to refer to the Formulas Chart on pages 181 and 182 if you need help during the real exam.

Example 1:

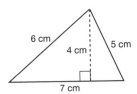

A. What is the perimeter of the triangle?

Perimeter = $side_1 + side_2 + side_3$

The lengths of the sides of the triangle are 7 cm, 6 cm, and 5 cm.

Perimeter = $side_1 + side_2 + side_3$
$= 7 + 6 + 5$
$= 18$

Answer: The perimeter of the triangle is 18 cm.

B. What is the area of the triangle?

Area = $\frac{1}{2} \times base \times height$

The base is the side on the bottom. The height is the distance from the top of the triangle to the base. The height is represented as a dashed line that is perpendicular to the base.

The base of the triangle is 7 cm, and the height is 4 cm.

Area = $\frac{1}{2} \times base \times height$
$= \frac{1}{2} \times 7 \times 4$
$= \frac{1}{2} \times 28$
$= \frac{28}{2}$
$= 14$

Answer: The area of the triangle is 14 square centimeters, or 14 cm².

Example 2:

A. What is the perimeter of the rectangle?

Perimeter = $2 \times length + 2 \times width$

The length of the rectangle is 12 in. The width is 7 in.

$$\begin{aligned}\text{Perimeter} &= 2 \times \text{length} + 2 \times \text{width}\\ &= 2 \times 12 + 2 \times 7\\ &= 24 + 14 \leftarrow \text{\footnotesize remember the order of}\\ & \qquad\qquad\qquad \text{\footnotesize operations (PEMDAS)}\\ &= 38\end{aligned}$$

Answer: The perimeter of the rectangle is 38 in.

B. What is the area of the rectangle?

$$\begin{aligned}\text{Area} &= \text{length} \times \text{width}\\ &= 12 \times 7\\ &= 84\end{aligned}$$

Answer: The area of the triangle is 84 square inches, or 84 in.^{2}.

Example 3: What is the area of the trapezoid?

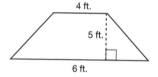

4 ft.

5 ft.

6 ft.

$$\text{Area} = \tfrac{1}{2} \times (\text{base}_1 + \text{base}_2) \times \text{height}$$

The bases of a trapezoid are the top and bottom sides. The height is the distance from the top base to the bottom base. The length of the top base is 4 ft, and the length of the bottom base is 6 ft. The height is 5 ft.

$$\begin{aligned}\text{Area} &= \tfrac{1}{2} \times (\text{base}_1 + \text{base}_2) \times \text{height}\\ &= \tfrac{1}{2} \times (4 + 6) \times 5\\ &= \tfrac{1}{2} \times 10 \times 5\\ &= \tfrac{1}{2} \times 50\\ &= \tfrac{50}{2}\\ &= 25\end{aligned}$$

Answer: The area of the trapezoid is 25 square feet or, 25 ft.^{2}.

Pythagorean Relationship

We can find the lengths of the sides of a right triangle using the formula for the **Pythagorean relationship**: $a^2 + b^2 = c^2$. In the formula, c represents the length of the hypotenuse. The **hypotenuse** is the longest side, which is always opposite the right angle. The letters a and b represent the lengths of the other two sides.

TIP

Like various formulas for area, perimeter, and volume, the Pythagorean formula will be available to you when you take the real GED® Math exam.

Example: What is the length of the hypotenuse of the right triangle?

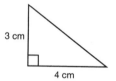

3 cm

4 cm

In the triangle above, $a = 3$ cm and $b = 4$ cm. We can use the Pythagorean relationship to find c, the length of the hypotenuse.

$$\begin{aligned}a^2 + b^2 &= c^2\\ 3^2 + 4^2 &= c^2\\ 9 + 16 &= c^2\\ 25 &= c^2\\ \sqrt{25} &= \sqrt{c^2} \leftarrow \text{\footnotesize recall that taking a square root of a}\\ & \qquad\qquad \text{\footnotesize number is the opposite of squaring a number}\\ 5 &= c\end{aligned}$$

Answer: The length of the hypotenuse is 5 cm.

Circles

A **circle** is a closed curve made up of points that are the same distance from the center. A line segment that passes through the center of the circle is called the **diameter**. A line segment that extends from the center to a point on the circle is called the **radius**. The radius is always two times the length of the diameter.

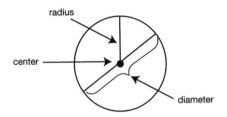

Circumference and Area

The **circumference** of a circle is the total distance around the circle. The area is the space inside the circle.

Circumference = π × diameter

Area = π × radius²

The symbol π (pi) has a value that is approximately equal to 3.14.

Example:

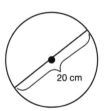

20 cm

A. What is the circumference of the circle?

Circumference = π × diameter

The diameter of the circle is 20 cm.

Circumference = π × diameter
$$\approx 3.14 \times 20$$
$$\approx 62.8$$

The symbol ≈ means "approximately equal to."

Answer: The circumference of the circle is approximately 62.8 cm.

B. What is the area of the circle?

Area = π × radius²

To find the area of the circle, we need to know the radius. The relationship between the diameter and the radius of a circle is Diameter = 2 × radius.

$$Diameter = 2 \times radius$$
$$20 = 2 \times radius$$
$$\frac{20}{2} = radius$$
$$10 = radius$$

The radius of the circle is 10 cm.

$$Area = \pi \times radius^2$$
$$\approx 3.14 \times 10^2$$
$$\approx 3.14 \times 100$$
$$\approx 314$$

Answer: The area of the circle is approximately 314 square centimeters, or 314 cm².

Solids

Solids are three-dimensional figures. Some common types of solids are shown here.

A cube has 6 square faces.

A rectangular solid has 6 rectangular faces.

A square pyramid has 4 triangular faces and a square base.

A cylinder has 2 circular bases.

A cone has 1 circular base.

Volume

Volume refers to the space inside a solid. The formulas for finding the volume of common solids are shown next.

Cube: Volume = edge^3

Rectangular solid: Volume = length × width × height

Square pyramid: Volume = $\frac{1}{3}$ × (base edge)^2 × height

Cylinder: Volume = π × radius^2 × height

Cone: Volume = $\frac{1}{3}$ × π × radius^2 × height

Example 1:

9 in.

What is the volume of the cube?

Volume = edge^3

The intersection of any two faces is called an **edge**. The edges of this cube are all 9 inches.

$$\text{Volume} = \text{edge}^3$$
$$= 9^3$$
$$= 729$$

Answer: The volume of the cube is 729 cubic in., or 729 in.^{3}.

Example 2:

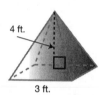

4 ft.

3 ft.

What is the volume of the square pyramid?

Volume = $\frac{1}{3}$ × (base edge)^2 × height

The base edge refers to the intersection of the base and a triangular face. The height is the distance from the top of the square pyramid to the base.

The base edge of the square pyramid is 3 ft. The height is 4 ft.

$$\text{Volume} = \frac{1}{3} \times (\text{base edge})^2 \times \text{height}$$
$$= \frac{1}{3} \times 3^2 \times 4$$
$$= \frac{1}{3} \times 9 \times 4$$
$$= \frac{1}{3} \times 36$$
$$= \frac{36}{3}$$
$$= 12$$

Answer: The volume of the square pyramid is 12 cubic ft., or 12 ft.^{3}.

Example 3:

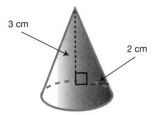

3 cm

2 cm

What is the volume of the cone?

$$\text{Volume} = \frac{1}{3} \times \pi \times \text{radius}^2 \times \text{height}$$

The radius of the circular base is 2 cm. The height, or distance from the top of the cone to the base, is 3 cm.

$$\text{Volume} = \frac{1}{3} \times \pi \times \text{radius}^2 \times \text{height}$$

$$\approx \frac{1}{3} \times 3.14 \times 2^2 \times 3$$

$$\approx \frac{1}{3} \times 3.14 \times 4 \times 3$$

$$\approx \frac{1}{3} \times 37.68$$

$$\approx 12.56$$

Answer: The volume of the cone is approximately 12.56 cubic cm, or 12.56 cm^3.

TIP

When solving a problem using formulas, keep your work organized and legible. Always write down the formula first. Then write the steps one below the other instead of to the right. Keep the equal signs lined up. And don't skip steps!

Quiz

1. Solve: 16 qt. = ☐ pt.
   a. 4
   b. 8
   c. 18
   d. 24
   e. 32

2. Which point on the number line represents −6.25?

   a. Point O
   b. Point P
   c. Point Q
   d. Point R
   e. Point S

3. Divide: $-100 \div -25$
   a. 75
   b. 10
   c. 4
   d. −4
   e. −75

4. What is the slope of the line that passes through $(-8,2)$ and $(4,7)$?
   a. $\frac{1}{6}$
   b. $\frac{2}{15}$
   c. $\frac{3}{10}$
   d. $\frac{4}{9}$
   e. $\frac{5}{12}$

5. Point *K* is located at (0,0). Point *L* is located at (4,1). What is the distance between Point *K* and Point *L*?

a. $\sqrt{3}$
b. $\sqrt{5}$
c. $\sqrt{6}$
d. $\sqrt{10}$
e. $\sqrt{17}$

6. Which pairs of angles are congruent?

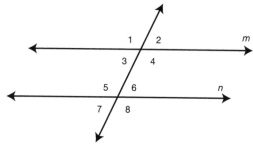

a. ∠1 and ∠6
b. ∠2 and ∠8
c. ∠3 and ∠6
d. ∠4 and ∠7
e. ∠7 and ∠8

7. What is *m*∠*T*?

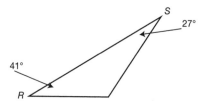

a. 14°
b. 22°
c. 68°
d. 112°
e. 292°

8. A square has side lengths of 8 in. What is the perimeter of the square?

a. 24 in.
b. 12 in.
c. 16 in.
d. 32 in.
e. 64 in.

9. A circle has a diameter of 6 cm. What is the approximate area of the circle in square centimeters?

10. What is the volume of the rectangular solid?

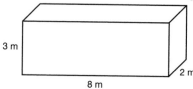

a. 13 m³
b. 16 m³
c. 24 m³
d. 48 m³
e. 64 m³

Quiz Answers

1. e. There are 2 pints in every quart, so $16 \times 2 = 32$ pints.

2. b. The most common incorrect answer on a problem like this is when people pick Point Q instead of Point P. This is because people are accustomed to reading from left to right, so they believe -7 would be to the right of -6. It's true that (positive) 7 is to the right of (positive) 6, but -7 is to the left of -6, so -6.25 would be Point P, not Point Q.

3. c. When two negative numbers are divided, the result is a positive number, so choice **c** is correct, not choice **d**. Any other answer would mean an error in division, or that subtraction was done instead of division.

4. e. With the two points given, plug the coordinates into the slope formula:

$$m = \frac{y_2 - y_1}{x_2 - x_1}$$
$$= \frac{7 - 2}{4 - (-8)}$$
$$= \frac{5}{12}$$

5. e. A sketch may help you tackle this problem better. One point is on the origin $(0,0)$, and the other is at $(4,1)$. You could draw a right triangle with these two points and a third point at $(4,0)$. If you do this, you can see that the Pythagorean formula can be used to find the distance between Points K and L, since that line is the hypotenuse of a right triangle.

$$a^2 + b^2 = c^2$$
$$4^2 + 1^2 = c^2$$
$$16 + 1 = c^2$$
$$17 = c^2$$
$$\sqrt{17} = c$$

You could also use the distance formula.

$$\text{distance between points} = \sqrt{(x_2 - x_1)^2 + (y_2 - y_1)^2}$$
$$= \sqrt{(4 - 0)^2 + (1 - 0)^2}$$
$$= \sqrt{4^2 + 1^2}$$
$$= \sqrt{16 + 1}$$
$$= \sqrt{17}$$

6. c. Recall that congruent angles have the same measurement. In the figure shown, angles 2, 3, 6, and 7 are all congruent with each other, and angles 1, 4, 5, and 8 are all congruent with each other.

7. d. There are two ways to approach this problem. Visually, figures are drawn to scale unless otherwise noted, and $m\angle T$ is greater than 90° (a right angle). This would make choices **d** and **e** your best guesses, and e is a rather large number, especially since the sum of all three interior angles in a triangle always equals 180°. Using this fact, you can determine: $180° - 41° - 27° = 112°$.

8. d. The formula for the perimeter of a square is $4s$.

Perimeter = 4(8)

Perimeter = 32 in

The answer is **d**. If you picked choice **e**, you found the area of the square.

9. To find the area of a circle, you must first use the diameter to find the radius.

Diameter = 2 × radius
       6 = 2 × radius
       3 = radius

The radius of the circle is 3 cm.

Area = $\pi \times radius^2$
    ≈ 3.14×3^2
    ≈ 3.14×9
    ≈ 28.26

The area of the circle is approximately 28.26 cm². This answer is still approximate because we used a simplified version of pi.

10. d. To find the volume of a rectangular solid, use the formula:

Volume = length × width × height
Volume = 8 × 2 × 3
Volume = 48

The volume of the rectangular solid is 48 m³.

Units of Measurement

To convert from a larger unit of measurement to a smaller unit (for example, from miles to yards), we multiply by the conversion factor. To convert from a smaller unit of measurement to a larger unit (for example, from grams to kilograms), we divide by the conversion factor.

Number Lines

Number lines can help us add and subtract positive and negative numbers. To add a positive number, we move to the right on the number line. To add negative numbers, we move to the left. To subtract a positive or negative number, we add its opposite.

Coordinate Plane

Given the coordinates of two points in a coordinate plane, we can find the distance between the points using the distance formula. We can also find the slope of the line that passes through the points using the slope formula.

Angles

Two angles are complementary if the sum of their measures is 90°. Two angles are supplementary if the sum of their measures is 180°. Congruent angles have the same measure.

Polygons

The sum of the measures of the interior angles in a triangle is 180°. The sum of the measures of the interior angles in a quadrilateral is 360°. The perimeter is the total distance around a polygon. The area is the space inside a polygon. The Pythagorean relationship refers to the relationship between the sides of a right triangle.

Circles

The circumference is the total distance around a circle. The area is the space inside a circle. The radius is the line segment from the center of the circle to any point on the circle. The diameter is twice the length of the radius and passes through the center of the circle, cutting it in half.

Solids

Solids are three-dimensional figures like cubes, rectangular solids, square pyramids, cylinders, and cones. The volume is the space inside a solid.

CHAPTER

5 ▶ DATA ANALYSIS

CHAPTER SUMMARY

This chapter will teach you how to read tables and graphs; how to calculate the mean, median, mode, and range of a set of data; and how to calculate the probability of an event.

Data is a set of numbers that gives us information about a situation. Many questions on the GED® Math exam will test your ability to analyze data. Analyzing data can involve finding probability, or reading charts and graphs.

Tables and Graphs

Tables

Tables list data in rows and columns. Rows are read from left to right, and columns are read from top to bottom.

Example: The following table shows data on 2009 median income by educational attainment. (We will learn more about the median of a data set in the next section.)

Median Income by Educational Attainment (1009)	
Educational Attainment	**Median Income**
Less than 9th grade	$19,386
9th to 12th, nongraduate	$22,222
High school graduate	$32,272
Some college, no degree	$40,387
Associate's degree	$44,757
Bachelor's degree or more	$62,394

Source: U.S. Census Bureau

A. What is the median income for a high school nongraduate?

First, we move down the "Educational Attainment" column to the row that reads "9th to 12th, nongraduate." Then we move to the right to the column labeled "Median Income."

Answer: The median income for a high school nongraduate is $22,222.

B. What is the median income for a high school graduate?

We move down the "Educational Attainment" column to the row that reads "High school graduate." Then we move to the right to the "Median Income" column.

Answer: The median income for a high school graduate is $32,272.

C. How much greater is the median income for a high school graduate than that for a high school nongraduate?

"How much greater" tells us to subtract the two median incomes.

$$\begin{array}{r} \$32,272 \\ -\$22,222 \\ \hline \$10,050 \end{array}$$

Answer: The median income for a high school graduate is $10,050 greater than for a high school nongraduate.

Line Graphs

Line graphs show changes in data over time. They are made up of points connected by **line segments**. Just like points on a coordinate plane, the location of each point on a line graph is determined by a pair of numbers. One number comes from the horizontal axis and the other number comes from the vertical axis.

Example: The following line graph shows the average sales price of new homes sold in the United States from 2000–2009.

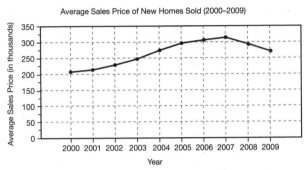

Average Sales Price of New Homes Sold (2000–2009)

Source: U.S. Census Bureau (line graph computer-generated).

A. During which year was the average sales price the highest?

The horizontal axis tells us the year, and the vertical axis tells us the average sales price in thousands. To find the highest average sales price, we find the highest point on the line. Then we move down to find the year.

> **Answer:** The year with the highest average sales price was 2007.

B. During which year or years was the average sales price approximately $275,000?

The label for the vertical axis reads "Average Sales Price (in thousands)." The part in parentheses tells us that the numbers along the vertical axis represent thousands. For example, $150 represents $150,000 and not $150.

To find $275,000, we move up the vertical axis until we reach $275. Then we move to the right until we reach the line. Be sure to look all the way across the graph, as the line may cross a certain value at multiple points.

> **Answer:** One year with the average sales price of approximately $275,000 is 2004. Note that another year with the same approximate median sale price is 2009.

C. What was the average sales price of new homes sold in 2005?

We move along the horizontal axis until we reach the year 2005. Then we move up until we reach the line. Finally, we move to the left to find the average sales price along the vertical axis.

> **Answer:** The average sales price of new homes sold in 2005 was approximately $300,000.

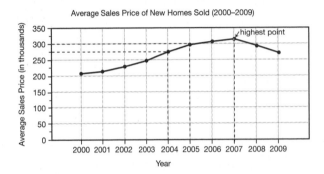

Average Sales Price of New Homes Sold (2000–2009)

Bar Graphs

Bar graphs are used to compare data. They are made up of rectangular bars of different sizes. Each bar represents a category, and the height of the bar tells us how much is in that category.

Example: The following bar graph shows the number of Representatives in the United States Congress for six states in 2011.

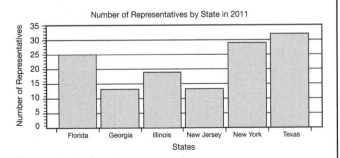

Number of Representatives by State in 2011

A. Which state has the greatest number of Representatives?

The horizontal axis tells us the different categories, or states. The vertical axis tells us the number of Representatives in each state. The state with the greatest number of Representatives will have the tallest bar.

Answer: Texas has the greatest number of Representatives.

B. Which states have the same number of Representatives?

The states with the same number of Representatives will have bars that are the same height.

Answer: Georgia and New Jersey have the same number of Representatives.

C. How many Representatives does Illinois have?

We start at the top of the bar for Illinois. Then we move to the left until we find the number of Representatives along the vertical axis.

Answer: Illinois has 19 Representatives.

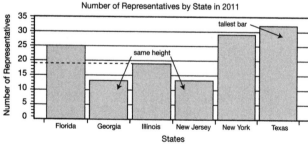

Source: www.house.gov (bar graph computer-generated).

Circle Graphs

A **circle graph**, also known as a pie chart, is used to show parts of a whole. It is made up of a circle that is divided into "slices." The circle represents the whole, and the slices represent parts of the whole. The slices are usually shown with percentages—the larger the slice, the larger the percentage. Together, the percentages add up to 100%.

Example: The following circle graph shows Kim's monthly budget.

A. Approximately what fraction of Kim's monthly income is spent on Household Expenses and Taxes?

The circle represents Kim's monthly budget, and the slices tell us how much Kim spends on each category. From the circle graph, we see that 24% of Kim's monthly income is spent on Household Expenses and

25% is spent on Taxes. We add to find the percent she spends on both.

$$24\% + 25\% = 49\%$$

We are asked to find an *approximate* fraction, so we can round 49% to 50%. Then we convert 50% to a fraction.

$$50\% = \frac{50}{100} = \frac{1}{2}$$

Answer: Approximately $\frac{1}{2}$ of Kim's monthly budget is spent on Household Expenses and Taxes.

B. If Kim earns $3,000 a month, how much does she save every month?

The circle graph tells us that Kim saves 15% every month. We need to convert 15% into a dollar amount. Recall from Chapter 1 that we can solve percent problems using the percent equation.

$$\begin{aligned}
\text{part} &= \text{percent} \times \text{whole} \\
&= 15\% \times 3{,}000 \\
&= 0.15 \times 3{,}000 \\
&= 450
\end{aligned}$$

Answer: Kim saves $450 a month.

Mean, Median, Mode, and Range

The mean, median, mode, and range are ways of describing data.

- The **mean** is the average of the values, or numbers, in a data set.

- The **median** is the middle value when all the values in a data set are arranged in order from least to greatest.
- The **mode** is the value that occurs most often in a data set.
- The **range** is the difference between the largest value and the smallest value in a data set.

Example 1: The table below shows Melody's work schedule for one week.

Melody's Work Schedule

Day	Number of Hours Worked
Monday	6
Tuesday	8
Wednesday	7
Thursday	5
Friday	5

A. What is the mean number of hours worked?

The formula for finding the mean of a data set is mean $= \frac{x_1 + x_2 + \dots + x_n}{n}$, where the x's represent the values in the data set and n represents the total number of values.

$$\begin{aligned}
\text{mean} &= \frac{x_1 + x_2 + \dots + x_n}{n} \\
&= \frac{6 + 8 + 7 + 5 + 5}{5} \quad \leftarrow \text{total number of hours worked} \\
&\qquad\qquad\qquad\quad \leftarrow \text{total number of days} \\
&= \frac{31}{5} \\
&= 6.2
\end{aligned}$$

Answer: The mean number of hours worked is 6.2.

When people usually talk about average, they are using the "mean" sense of the word. This is the type of average seen most often in newspapers, magazines, and so forth, so chances are that you are familiar with the mean as an average even if you are unfamiliar with this term.

B. What is the median number of hours worked?

To find the median, we first list the values in order from least to greatest. Then we find the value that is in the middle.

middle value
↓
5 5 6 7 8

Answer: The median number of hours worked is 6.

C. What is the mode?

To find the mode, we look for the value that occurs most often.

$\boxed{5\ 5}$ 6 7 8

Answer: The mode is 5.

D. What is the range?

To find the range, we subtract the highest value and the lowest value.

$8 - 5 = 3$

Answer: The range is 3.

Example 2: Suppose Melody also worked 8 hours on Saturday.

A. What effect does the change in data have on the mean number of hours worked?

The data set now includes an additional 8 hours on Saturday, so we add 8 to the numerator. The denominator increases by 1 since the total number of days is now 6 instead of 5.

$$\text{mean} = \frac{x_1 + x_2 + \ldots + x_n}{n}$$

$$= \frac{6 + 8 + 7 + 5 + 5 + 8}{6} \quad \begin{array}{l} \leftarrow \text{add 8 to the numerator} \\ \leftarrow \text{denominator increases by 1} \end{array}$$

$$= \frac{39}{6}$$

$$= 6.5$$

Answer: The mean number of hours worked increased from 6.2 to 6.5 when we added 8 to the data set.

B. What effect does the change in data have on the median number of hours worked?

When we order the values from least to greatest, we find that we no longer have a given value that is exactly in the middle. Instead, the middle value is now halfway between 6 and 7.

middle value
↓
5 5 6   7 8 8

To find the median when you have a situation like this (an even number of values), you take the two middle values and find the mean of those values.

$$\text{mean} = \frac{x_1 + x_2 + \ldots + x_n}{n}$$

$$= \frac{6 + 7}{2}$$

$$= \frac{13}{2}$$

$$= 6.5$$

Answer: The median number of hours worked increased from 6 to 6.5 when we added 8 to the data set.

C. What effect does the change in data have on the mode?

There are now two values that occur most often.

$$\boxed{5\ 5}\ \ 6\ \ 7\ \ \boxed{8\ 8}$$

Answer: The data set now has two modes, 5 and 8.

D. What is the range?

Even though we added an additional value to the data set, the highest value is still 8 and the lowest value is still 5.

Answer: The range did not change when we added 8 to the data set.

TIP

Here is one way to remember the difference between mean, median, and mode:

It is "mean" to call someone "average."

The word "median" sounds like "medium," and a medium-sized shirt is the middle size.

The words "mode" and "most" both begin with "mo-."

Probability

The **probability** of an event tells us how likely the event is to occur. We can use the probability of an event to make predictions.

Experimental Probability

The **experimental probability** of an event is its estimated probability based on data. It is calculated as the ratio of the number of times the event occurs to the total number of outcomes.

$$\text{Experimental probability} = \frac{\text{number of times the event occurs}}{\text{total number of outcomes}}$$

Example: Joey repeatedly draws a marble at random from a bag and then replaces it. The following table shows the number of times Joey draws a marble of each color.

Results of Drawing Marbles at Random	
Color	**Number of Times**
Red	4
Orange	8
Yellow	3
Blue	9

A. Based on the data, what is the probability of drawing a red marble?

First, we add to find the total number of times Joey randomly drew a marble from the bag:

$$4 + 8 + 3 + 9 = 24$$

The total number of outcomes is 24. The number of times he drew a red marble is 4.

Experimental probability

$$= \frac{\text{number of times the event occurs}}{\text{total number of outcomes}} = \frac{4}{24} = \frac{1}{6}$$

Answer: Based on the data, the probability of drawing a red marble is $\frac{1}{6}$.

B. If Joey randomly draws another 30 marbles, about how many times should he expect to draw a red marble?

To predict the number of red marbles, we multiply the number of marbles to be drawn by the probability of drawing a red marble.

$$30 \times \frac{1}{6} = \frac{30}{1} \times \frac{1}{6} = \frac{30}{6} = 5$$

Answer: If Joey randomly draws another 30 marbles, he should expect to draw a red marble about 5 times.

Theoretical Probability

The **theoretical probability** of an event is the expected probability based on what *should* occur. It is calculated as the ratio of the number of favorable outcomes to the total number of possible outcomes.

Theoretical probability $= \dfrac{\text{number of favorable outcomes}}{\text{total number of possible outcomes}}$

Example: The following spinner is divided into eight equal parts.

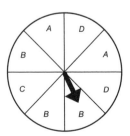

A. What is the probability that the pointer will land on the letter *B*?

The spinner is divided into eight equal parts, so there are a total of 8 possible outcomes. We are interested in the pointer landing on the letter *B*. Since there are three *B*s on the spinner, the number of favorable outcomes is 3.

Theoretical probability

$$= \frac{\text{number of favorable outcomes}}{\text{total number of possible outcomes}} = \frac{3}{8}$$

Answer: The probability of the pointer landing on *B* is $\frac{3}{8}$.

B. If the spinner is spun 10 times, what is the best prediction of the number of times the pointer will land on *B*?

To predict the number of times the pointer will land on *B*, we multiply.

$$10 \times \frac{3}{8} = \frac{10}{1} \times \frac{3}{8} = \frac{30}{8} = 3.75$$

It does not make sense to say that the pointer will land on *B* 3.75 times. A reasonable answer would be a whole number, so we round 3.75 to the nearest whole number.

Answer: If the spinner is spun 10 times, the pointer will land on *B* approximately 4 times.

Quiz

The line graph below shows the population of Austin, TX, from 1950–2000.

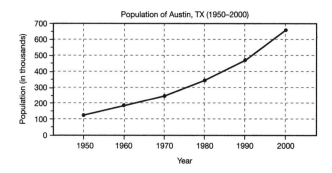

1. What was the approximate population of Austin, TX, in 1980?

a. 150,000

b. 200,000

c. 250,000

d. 300,000

e. 350,000

2. Approximately how much greater was the population in 1980 than in 1970?

a. 100,000

b. 200,000

c. 300,000

d. 400,000

e. 500,000

3. Which conclusion can be drawn about the population of Austin from 1950–2000?

a. The population did not change.

b. The population increased over time.

c. The population decreased over time.

d. The population increased and then decreased.

e. The population decreased and then increased.

The following circle graph shows the percent of each type of doctor at a medical clinic.

4. What fraction of the doctors are allergists?

a. $\frac{1}{2}$

b. $\frac{1}{4}$

c. $\frac{1}{5}$

d. $\frac{1}{10}$

e. $\frac{1}{20}$

5. If there are 50 doctors at the clinic, how many are pediatricians?

a. 5

b. 9

c. 10

d. 11

e. 15

The following table shows the total number of medals won by five Olympic athletes.

Medal Winners	
Athlete	**Total Number of Medals**
Nicole	15
Larisa	23
Michael	16
Boris	13
Takashi	13

Source: http://www.sports-reference.com/olympics/.

6. What is the mean of the data?

    a. 12.5

    b. 13

    c. 15

    d. 15.5

    e. 16

7. What is the median of the data?

    a. 13

    b. 15

    c. 15.5

    d. 16

    e. 18

8. What is the mode of the data?

    a. 13

    b. 15

    c. 15.5

    d. 16

    e. 18

Jackie tosses a coin 20 times and records the number of times the coin lands on heads and on tails. The following table shows her data.

Results of Coin Toss	
Outcome	**Number of Times**
Heads	12
Tails	8

9. Based on the data, what is the probability that the coin will land on heads?

    a. $\frac{1}{3}$

    b. $\frac{1}{4}$

    c. $\frac{2}{3}$

    d. $\frac{2}{5}$

    e. $\frac{3}{5}$

10. If Jackie tosses the coin 30 more times, about how many times should she expect the coin to land on heads?

Quiz Answers

1. e. To read this graph correctly, first look along the horizontal axis and find the year 1980. Then proceed up until you hit the line graph. Looking left to the vertical axis, you can see that this point is between 300,000 and 400,000, making 350,000 the best estimate.

2. a. From the first question, you know the population in 1980 was roughly 350,000. If you follow the same procedure as above to find the population in 1970, you see that it is roughly between 200,000 and 300,000, or 250,000. To find the difference between the populations in 1980 and 1970, subtract the two values: 350,000 − 250,000 = 100,000.

3. b. The line graph trends upward at all points on the graph. This corresponds to an increase in population over the entire time period in question.

4. c. Although this technically a data analysis question, it requires you to have correct knowledge of number sense concepts, specifically fractions and percentages. This will often be the case, as many questions involve more than just a single math standard or idea.

    If you are unsure how to convert a percentage into a fraction, refer back to the section in Chapter 1 that discusses this. The slice of the circle graph that represents allergists takes up 20% of the circle. 20% means "20 out of 100," so it can be written—and then reduced by dividing both the numerator and denominator by 20 (the GCF)—the following way:

$$\frac{20}{100} = \frac{20 \div 20}{100 \div 20} = \frac{1}{5}$$

5. d. The percentage of pediatricians is 22%, which can be converted to the decimal 0.22. Multiplying 50 by 0.22 gives you:

$50 \times 0.22 = 11$ pediatricians

    You could also find the answer by converting the percentage to a fraction. Like in Question 4, 22% becomes: $\frac{22}{100}$, or $\frac{11}{50}$. The latter value comes after you reduce the fraction.

    If you multiply this value by 50, you get:

$\frac{11}{50} \times 50 = 11$ pediatricians

6. e. To find the mean, you must add up the number of medals won, and then divide by the total number of athletes.

$\frac{15 + 23 + 16 + 13 + 13}{5} = \frac{80}{5} = 16$ medals

7. b. To find the median of a set of numbers, recall that you list the numbers from least to greatest and then determine the middle value.

13   13   15   16   23

The middle value is 15, so this is the median.

8. a. The mode is the value that occurs most often in a set. Sometimes a set of data will not have a mode, and other times it may have more than one mode. However, in this set, two people won 13 medals, so 13 is the mode.

9. e. Most people understand that a coin has two sides, so the probability of one side landing up is typically $\frac{1}{2}$. However, if you were to base a probability on the table shown, you would see that heads comes up more times than tails. The coin was tossed 20 times, and heads appeared 12 times. Perhaps, over time, this would even out, but based on the table shown, the probability would be:

$\frac{12}{20} = \frac{3}{5}$

10. Answer:

1	8			
	⊘	⊘	⊘	
⊙	⊙	⊙	⊙	⊙

Since the probability of the coin landing on heads is known ($\frac{3}{5}$), all that needs to be done is to multiply this probability by 30.

$\frac{3}{5} \times 30 = 18$

Tables and Graphs

Tables and graphs are ways of organizing and displaying data.

Tables list data in rows and columns.

Line graphs show changes in data over time.

Bar graphs are used to compare data.

Circle graphs are used to show parts of a whole.

Mean, Median, Mode, and Range

The mean, median, mode, and range are ways of describing data.

The mean is the average of the data.

The median is the middle value.

The mode is the value that occurs the most often.

The range is the difference between the highest value and the lowest value.

Probability

The probability of an event is a ratio that compares the number of times an event occurred (or *should* occur) to the total number of outcomes. We can use the probability of an event to make predictions about the number of times an event will occur.

CHAPTER

6 ▶ ALGEBRA

CHAPTER SUMMARY
The objective of this chapter is to help you identify algebraic expressions and solve algebraic equations and proportions. It will also teach you how to use the equation of a line and other important algebraic formulas.

Algebra is the branch of mathematics that denotes quantities with letters and uses negative numbers as well as ordinary numbers. You often use algebra to translate everyday situations into a math sentence so that you can then solve problems. This is the reason why the GED® Math exam will test your knowledge of Algebra skills and concepts.

Algebraic Expressions

In Chapters 3 and 4, we used  to represent a number that we wanted to solve for. In this chapter, we will use a letter, such as x, instead of ⟨?⟩. The letter x is called a **variable** and is used to represent an unknown number.

Math phrases that contain numbers, variables, and operation signs are called **algebraic expressions**.

Writing Algebraic Expressions

It is important to learn how to translate words into algebraic expressions. The following table shows examples of word phrases for each type of expression.

Operation	Word Phrases	Expression	Word Phrases	Expression
Addition	add 7 to n sum of n and 7 7 more than n n increased by 7 n plus 7	$n + 7$ or $7 + n$		
Subtraction	subtract 4 from x 4 subtracted from x difference of x and 4 4 less than x x minus 4	$x - 4$	subtract x from 4 x subtracted from 4 difference of 4 and x 4 minus x	$4 - x$
Multiplication	3 multiplied by p 3 times p product of 3 and p	$3p$		
Division	11 divided into a a divided by 11 quotient of a and 11	$a \div 11$ or $\frac{a}{11}$	a divided into 11 11 divided by a quotient of 11 and a	$11 \div a$ or $\frac{11}{a}$

Example 1: Write each phrase as an algebraic expression:

A. difference of y and 19

The words "difference of" tell us to subtract.

Answer: $y - 19$

B. v divided by 35

The words "divided by" tell us to divide.

Answer: $v \div 35$ or $\frac{v}{35}$

C. 23 more than k

The words "more than" tell us to add.

Answer: $k + 23$

D. 45 multiplied by w

The words "multiplied by" tell us to multiply.

Answer: $45w$

Example 2: Write each phrase as an algebraic expression:

A. 5 more than the product of 9 and f

There are two operations in the math phrase:

$$\underbrace{\text{5 more than}}_{5+} \text{ the } \underbrace{\text{product of 9 and } f}_{9f}$$

Answer: $5 + 9f$

B. 10 times the difference of j and 1

$$\underbrace{\text{10 times}}_{10\times} \text{ the } \underbrace{\text{difference of } j \text{ and } 1}_{(j-1)}$$

We learned in Chapter 1 that the order of operations is parentheses, exponents, multiplication, division, addition, and subtraction (PEMDAS). We put parentheses around $j - 1$ to show that we need to subtract 1 from j BEFORE we multiply by 10.

Answer: $10 \times (j - 1)$ or $10(j - 1)$

Without the parentheses, the algebraic expression above would be $10j - 1$, or "1 less than the product of 10 and j."

Evaluating Algebraic Expressions

We can evaluate algebraic expressions if we are given the value of the variable.

Example 1:

A. Find the value of $6x$ when $x = 12$.

To evaluate $6x$ when $x = 12$, we replace x with 12 and multiply.

$$6x = 6 \times 12 = 72$$

Answer: $6x = 72$ when $x = 12$

B. Find the value of $6x$ when $x = 9$.

We replace x with 9 and multiply.

$$6x = 6 \times 9 = 54$$

Answer: $6x = 54$ when $x = 9$

Example 2: Find the value of $3b + 6(c + 2)$ when $b = 0$ and $c = 8$.

We replace b with 0 and c with 8. Since there is more than one operation in the expression, we apply the order of operations.

$$\begin{aligned}
3b + 6(c + 2) &= 3(0) + 6(8 + 2) \\
&= 3(0) + 6(10) \\
&= 0 + 60 \\
&= 60
\end{aligned}$$

Answer: $3b + 6(c + 2) = 60$ when $b = 0$ and $c = 8$

Simplifying Algebraic Expressions

Simplifying an algebraic expression means to write the expression in simplest form. We can simplify algebraic expressions by combining like terms and using the Distributive Property.

Combining Like Terms

Terms are the parts of an expression that are separated by $+$ and $-$ signs. **Like terms** are terms that have the same variable. For example, the following algebraic expression has 5 terms: $3n$, $4n$, $2p$, p, and 5. The terms $3n$ and $4n$ are like terms because they both have the same variable, n. The terms $2p$ and p are also like terms because they both contain the same variable, p.

$$\overbrace{3n \ + \ 4n}^{\text{like terms}} \underbrace{- \ 2p \ - \ p}_{\text{like terms}} + 5$$

Example:

A. Simplify: $7x + 2x + 1$

The terms $7x$ and $2x$ can be combined because they both have the variable x. When we add two like terms, we add the numbers in front of the variable.

$$\overbrace{7x + 2x}^{\text{like terms}} + 1 = \boxed{7}x + \boxed{2}x + 1$$

$$= \boxed{9}x + 1$$

We can visualize this as adding 2 x's to 7 x's.

$$\overbrace{7x + 2x}^{\text{like terms}} + 1 = \overbrace{\boxed{x}\,\boxed{x}\,\boxed{x}\,\boxed{x}\,\boxed{x}\,\boxed{x}\,\boxed{x}}^{7x} + \overbrace{\boxed{x}\,\boxed{x}}^{2x} + 1$$

$$= \overbrace{\boxed{x}\,\boxed{x}\,\boxed{x}\,\boxed{x}\,\boxed{x}\,\boxed{x}\,\boxed{x}\,\boxed{x}\,\boxed{x}}^{9x} + 1$$

Answer: $7x + 2x + 1 = 9x + 1$

B. Simplify: $6t - 3t - 2s$

The terms $6t$ and $3t$ can be combined because they both have the variable t. When we subtract two like terms, we subtract the numbers in front of the variable.

$$\overbrace{6t - 3t}^{\text{like terms}} - 2s = \boxed{6}t - \boxed{3}t - 2s$$

$$= \boxed{3}t - 2s$$

We can visualize this as taking 3 t's away from 6 t's.

$$\overbrace{6t - 3t}^{\text{like terms}} - 2s = \overbrace{\boxed{t}\,\boxed{t}\,\boxed{t}\,\underbrace{\boxed{t}\,\boxed{t}\,\boxed{t}}_{3t}}^{6t} - \overbrace{\boxed{s}\,\boxed{s}}^{2s}$$

$$= \overbrace{\boxed{t}\,\boxed{t}\,\boxed{t}}^{3t} - \overbrace{\boxed{s}\,\boxed{s}}^{2s}$$

Answer: $6t - 3t - 2s = 3t - 2s$

C. Simplify: $3n + 4n - 2p - p + 5$

We learned in Chapter 2 that we can subtract a positive or negative number by adding its opposite. For example, we can evaluate $-5 - 1$ by rewriting it as $-5 + (-1)$. We can also rewrite subtraction as addition in the algebraic expression.

$$3n + 4n - 2p - p + 5 = 3n + 4n + (-2p) + (-1p) + 5 \quad \leftarrow \text{ rewrite the subtraction as addition}$$

$$= \boxed{3}n + \boxed{4}n + (-2p) + (-1p) + 5$$

$$= \boxed{7}n + (-2p) + (-1p) + 5$$

$$= 7n + \boxed{-2}p + \boxed{-1}p + 5$$

$$= 7n + \boxed{-3}p + 5$$

$$= 7n - 3p + 5$$

Answer: $3n + 4n - 2p - p + 5 = 7n - 3p + 5$

Distributive Property

The **Distributive Property** states that the sum of two numbers, $b + c$, multiplied by another number, a, is equal to the sum of $a \times b$ and $a \times c$. The Distributive Property also applies when we subtract b and c.

$$a(b + c) = \overset{a \times b}{a(b + c)} = ab + ac \quad a(b - c) = \overset{a \times b}{a(b - c)} = ab - ac$$

Example 1:

A. Simplify: $2(5k + 1)$

The expression is in the form $a(b + c)$, so we can apply the Distributive Property.

$$\overset{a(b+c)}{2(5k + 1)} = \overset{2}{2 \times 5k} + \underset{2}{2 \times 1}$$

To multiply $2 \times 5k$, we multiply the whole numbers:

$$2 \times 5k + 2 = \boxed{2} \times \boxed{5}k + 2$$
$$= \boxed{10}k + 2$$

We can visualize this as adding 2 groups of $5k$.

$$2 \times 5k + 2 = \overset{5k}{\boxed{k\,k\,k\,k\,k}} + \overset{5k}{\boxed{k\,k\,k\,k\,k}} + 2$$
$$= \overset{10k}{\boxed{k\,k\,k\,k\,k\,k\,k\,k\,k\,k}} + 2$$

Answer: $2(5k + 1) = 10k + 2$

B. Simplify: $8(m - n)$

The expression is in the form $a(b - c)$, so we can apply the Distributive Property.

$$\overset{a(b-c)}{8(m - n)} = 8m - 8n$$

There are no like terms in this expression, so it can't be simplified further.

Answer: $8(m - n) = 8m - 8n$

Example 2: Simplify: $9w + 5y - 3(y + w)$

According to the order of operations, we perform operations involving parentheses and multiplication before we add and subtract. Although there are parentheses in this expression, there are no like terms inside them, so we can't actually perform an operation. Multiplication is next, and the part of the expression with parentheses is in the form $a(b + c)$, so we apply the Distributive Property first.

$$9w + 5y - 3(y + w) = 9w + 5y + \overset{a(b+c)}{(-3)(y + w)} \leftarrow \text{rewrite the subtraction as addition}$$
$$= 9w + 5y + (-3y) + (-3w)$$
$$= 9w + (-3w) + 5y + (-3y) \leftarrow \text{move like terms next to each other}$$
$$= 6w + 2y$$

Answer: $9w + 5y - 3(y + w) = 6w + 2y$

Algebraic Equations

When we write an algebraic expression followed by an equal sign and a number, we have an **algebraic equation**.

Algebraic Expression	Algebraic Equation
$j + 16$	$j + 16 = 25$

Writing Algebraic Equations

We translate words into algebraic equations the same way we translate words into expressions. The difference is that the word "is" tells us to write an equation, not an expression. The word "is" represents the equal sign.

Example: Write "the quotient of h and 10 is 0.4" as an algebraic equation.

The word "quotient" tells us to divide. The word "is" tells us that the quotient is equal to 0.4.

Answer: $h \div 10 = 0.4$ or $\frac{h}{10} = 0.4$

Solving Algebraic Equations

To solve an algebraic equation means to find the value of the variable that makes the equation true. We use **inverse operations** and the **Properties of Equality** to help us solve equations.

Inverse operations "undo" each other. We use inverse operations to get a variable by itself.

Inverse Operations	Example	Example
Addition and subtraction are inverse operations	$w + 2$ $2 + 2 - 2 \leftarrow$ subtract 2 to undo $+ 2$ $w + (2 - 2)$ $w + 0$ w	$w - 4$ $w - 4 + 4 \leftarrow$ add 4 to undo $- 4$ $w + (-4) + 4$ $w + (-4 + 4)$ $w + 0$ w
Multiplication and division are inverse operations	$5w \leftarrow$ Think: $w \times 5$ $\frac{5w}{5} \leftarrow$ divide by 5 to undo $\times 5$ $\frac{\boxed{5}w}{\boxed{5}} \leftarrow$ divide the whole numbers $1w$ w	$\frac{w}{3} \leftarrow$ Think: $w \div 3$ $\frac{3w}{3} \leftarrow$ multiply by 3 to undo $\div 3$ $\frac{\boxed{3}w}{\boxed{3}} \leftarrow$ divide the whole numbers $1w$ w

The Properties of Equality keep both sides of an equation equal.

Properties of Equality	Example
Additional Property of Equality: If we add the same number to both sides of an equation, the two sides remain equal.	$4 - 1 = 3$ $4 - 1 + 1 = 3 + 1$ ← add 1 to both sides $4 + 0 = 4$ $4 = 4$
Subtraction Property of Equality: If we subtract the same number from both sides of an equation, the two sides remain equal.	$3 + 2 = 5$ $3 + 2 - 2 = 5 - 2$ ← subtract 2 from both sides $3 + 0 = 3$ $3 = 3$
Multiplication Property of Equality: If we multiply both sides of an equation by the same number, the two sides remain equal.	$8 + 2 = 10$ $(8 + 2) \times 6 = 10 \times 6$ ← multiply both sides by 6 $10 \times 6 = 60$ $60 = 60$
Division Property of Equality: If we divide both sides of an equation by the same number, the two sides remain equal.	$4 \times 3 = 12$ $\frac{4 \times 3}{2} = \frac{12}{2}$ ← divide both sides by 2 $\frac{12}{2} = 6$ $6 = 6$

If we do not add, subtract, multiply, or divide on both sides of the equation, the two sides will no longer be equal. For example:

$$3 + 2 = 5$$
$$3 + 2 - 2 \neq 5 \leftarrow \text{subtract from only one side}$$
$$3 + 0 \neq 5$$
$$3 \neq 5$$

Example 1:

A. Solve: $j + 16 = 25$

To solve the equation, we need j by itself on one side of the equal sign. Since this is an addition equation, we use subtraction to undo the addition. Then we use the Subtraction Property of Equality to keep both sides equal.

$$j + 16 = 25$$
$$j + 16 - 16 = 25 - 16 \leftarrow \text{use the inverse of addition and the Subtraction Property of Equality}$$
$$\uparrow \qquad \uparrow$$
$$j + 0 = 9$$
$$j = 9$$

Answer: $j = 9$

B. Solve: $n - 22 = 30$

The equation is a subtraction equation, so we use addition to undo the subtraction and the Addition Property of Equality to keep both sides equal.

$$n - 22 = 30$$
$$n - 22 + 22 = 30 + 22 \leftarrow \text{use the inverse of subtraction and the Addition Property of Equality}$$
$$\uparrow \qquad\qquad \uparrow$$
$$n + 0 = 52$$
$$n = 52$$

Answer: $n = 52$

C. Solve: $7r = 21$

The equation is a multiplication equation, so we use division to undo the multiplication and the Division Property of Equality to keep both sides equal.

$$7r = 21$$
$$\frac{7r}{7} = \frac{21}{7} \leftarrow \text{use the inverse of multiplication and the Division Property of Equality}$$
$$1 \times r = 3$$
$$r = 3$$

Answer: $r = 3$

D. $\frac{r}{11} = 4$

The equation is a division equation, so we use multiplication to undo the division and the Multiplication Property of Equality to keep both sides equal.

$$\frac{r}{11} = 4$$
$$\frac{11r}{11} = 4 \times 11 \leftarrow \text{use the inverse of division and the Multiplication Property of Equality}$$
$$1 \times r = 44$$
$$r = 44$$

Answer: $r = 44$

Example 2: Solve: $10z + 3 = 20$

The equation has two operations, addition and multiplication, so we will need to use two inverse operations and two Properties of Equality to solve for z.

We use the inverse of addition and the Subtraction Property of Equality to get $10z$ by itself on one side of the equal sign. Then we use the inverse of multiplication and the Division Property of Equality to get z by itself.

$$10z + 3 = 20$$
$$10z + 3 - 3 = 20 - 3 \leftarrow \text{use the inverse of addition and the Subtraction Property of Equality}$$
$$10z + 0 = 17$$
$$10z = 17 \leftarrow \text{10z is by itself}$$
$$\frac{10z}{10} = \frac{17}{10} \leftarrow \text{use the inverse of multiplication and the Division Property of Equality}$$
$$1 \times z = 1.7$$
$$z = 1.7$$

Answer: $z = 1.7$

Example 3: Solve: $5s - 8 + 2s = 27$

To solve for s, we will need to simplify the algebraic expression first by combining like terms. Then we use inverse operations and the Properties of Equality.

$$5s - 8 + 2s = 27$$
$$\boxed{5}s + \boxed{2}s - 8 = 27 \leftarrow \text{move like terms next to each other}$$
$$7s - 8 = 27$$
$$7s - 8 + 8 = 27 + 8 \leftarrow \text{use the inverse of subtraction and the Addition Property of Equality}$$
$$7s + (-8) + 8 = 27 + 8$$
$$7s + 0 = 35$$
$$7s = 35 \leftarrow \text{7s by itself}$$
$$\frac{7s}{7} = \frac{35}{7} \leftarrow \text{use the inverse of multiplication and the Division Property of Equality}$$
$$s = 5$$

Answer: $s = 5$

Equation of a Line

We learned in Chapter 2 that a point on a coordinate plane is represented by an ordered pair of numbers (x,y). We also learned that we can draw a straight line that passes through two points. The line can be represented by an algebraic equation. If we know the equation, we can graph the line on a coordinate plane.

Example: A line is represented by the equation $y = 2x - 1$. What is the graph of the line?

To graph the line, we need to create a table of x and y values. We start by choosing the values of x that we want to use in the equation.

x	2x–1	y	(x,y)
–2			
–1			
0			
1			
2			

Then we use our x values to solve for the y values. For example, when $x = -2$:

$$y = 2x - 1$$
$$= 2(-2) - 1$$
$$= -4 - 1$$
$$= -5$$

x	2x–1	y	(x,y)
–2	2(–2) – 1	–5	
–1	2(–1) – 1	–3	
0	2(0) – 1	–1	
1	2(1) – 1	1	
2	2(2) – 1	3	

The x and y values represent the x-coordinates and y-coordinates of five points on the line.

x	2x–1	y	(x,y)
–2	2(–2) – 1	–5	(–2,–5)
–1	2(–1) – 1	–3	(–1,–3)
0	2(0) – 1	–1	(0,–1)
1	2(1) – 1	1	(1,1)
2	2(2) – 1	3	(2,3)

We plot the ordered pairs on the coordinate plane and draw a straight line through those points. Draw arrows on the ends of the line to indicate that the line extends to infinity in both directions.

Answer:

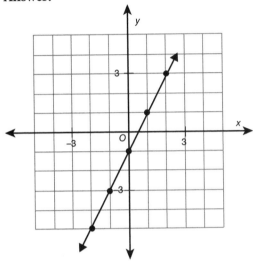

TIP

When you create a table of x and y values, always choose small values for x. This will make it easier to solve for y. For example, you can choose –2, –1, 0, 1, and 2 to replace x in the equation y = 6x + 3. You can also choose 0, 1, 2, and 3. You will end up with the same line on the coordinate plane. If you choose 11, 12, 13, and 14, you will also end up with the same line, but it will be harder to solve for y!

Formulas

Recall from Chapter 2 that the formula for the area of a rectangle is Area = length × width. We can rewrite the formula using variables instead of words. If A = area, l = length, and w = width, then the formula for the area of a rectangle is $A = l \times w$.

We learned to solve for A, the area, by multiplying the values for length and width. But what if we want to solve for the width? We use inverse operations and the Properties of Equality.

Example: The area of the following rectangle is 45 cm². What is w, the width of the rectangle?

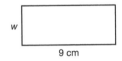

The formula for the area of a rectangle is $A = l \times w$. We know that $A = 45$ cm² and $l = 9$ cm. To solve for w, we use the inverse of multiplication and the Division Property of Equality.

$$A = l \times w$$
$$45 = 9w$$
$$\frac{45}{9} = \frac{9w}{9}$$
$$5 = w$$

Answer: The width of the rectangle is 5 cm.

Proportions

We learned in Chapter 1 that a proportion is an equation that shows two equivalent ratios. When there is a variable in the proportion, we cross multiply. Then we use the inverse of multiplication and the Division Property of Equality to solve for the variable.

Example: Solve: $\frac{3}{15} = \frac{2}{p}$

$$\frac{3}{15} = \frac{2}{p}$$

$\overbrace{3 \times p}^{\text{cross product 1}} = \overbrace{2 \times 15}^{\text{cross product 2}}$

$$3p = 30$$
$$\frac{3p}{3} = \frac{30}{3}$$
$$p = 10$$

Answer: $p = 10$

Rates

A **rate** is a ratio in which the second number is always a 1. The following are examples of rates:

$$\frac{50 \text{ miles}}{1 \text{ hour}} \qquad \frac{\$1.25}{1 \text{ pound}} \qquad \frac{70 \text{ words}}{1 \text{ minute}}$$

We can also express rates using the word "per":

50 miles per hour $1.25 per pound
70 words per minute

We can use proportions to solve problems involving rates.

> **Example:** A car travels at 50 miles per hour. How long will it take to travel 100 miles?

Let h = the number of hours it will take to travel 100 miles. Since 50 miles per hour is a rate, we set up a proportion to solve for h.

rate → $\dfrac{50 \text{ miles}}{1 \text{ hour}} = \dfrac{100 \text{ miles}}{h}$ ←distance traveled
←the number of hours it will take to travel 100 miles

Notice that the unit of measurement in the numerators must be the same (miles). The unit of measurement in the denominators must also be the same (hours).

$$\frac{50}{1} = \frac{100}{h}$$
$$50 \times h = 100 \times 1$$
$$50h = 100$$
$$\frac{50h}{50} = \frac{100}{50}$$
$$h = 2$$

Answer: It will take 2 hours for the car to travel 100 miles.

Scale Drawings

A **scale** is a ratio of the measure of an object in a drawing to the actual measure of that object. A scale allows us to create drawings that are proportional to the actual object.

> **Example:** The diagram below shows a scale drawing of a room. The scale is 1 inch:8 feet.

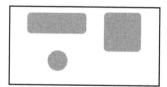

If the length of the room in the drawing is 2 inches, what is the actual length of the room?

Let L = the actual length of the room. Since a scale is a ratio, we can write the scale in fraction form. Then we set up a proportion to solve for L.

$$\text{scale} \rightarrow \frac{1 \text{ inch}}{8 \text{ feet}} = \frac{2 \text{ inches}}{L} \begin{array}{l} \leftarrow\text{length of the room in the scale drawing} \\ \leftarrow\text{actual length of the room} \end{array}$$

$$\frac{1}{8} = \frac{2}{L}$$
$$1 \times L = 2 \times 8$$
$$L = 16$$

Answer: The actual length of the room is 16 feet.

Similar Polygons

Similar polygons are polygons that have the same shape but not necessarily the same size. Two polygons are similar if the lengths of their corresponding sides are proportional and their corresponding angles are congruent.

The following table shows examples of similar polygons and their corresponding sides.

Similar Polygons	Corresponding Sides
	side *AB* and side *DE* are corresponding sides side *BC* and side *EF* are corresponding sides side *AC* and side *DF* are corresponding sides
	side *ST* and side *WX* are corresponding sides side *TU* and side *XY* are corresponding sides side *UV* and side *YZ* are corresponding sides side *SV* and side *WZ* are corresponding sides
	side *KL* and side *OP* are corresponding sides side *LM* and side *PQ* are corresponding sides side *MN* and side *QR* are corresponding sides side *KN* and side *OR* are corresponding sides

Example: Triangle *ABC* is similar to triangle *RST*. What is *s*, the length of side *AB*?

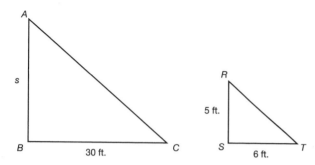

From the diagram, we see that side *AB* and side *RS* are corresponding sides. Side *BC* and side *ST* are also corresponding sides. Since the lengths of the corresponding sides of two similar polygons are proportional, we set up a proportion to solve for *s*.

corresponding sides → $\dfrac{AB}{RS} = \dfrac{BC}{ST}$ ← corresponding sides

$$\frac{AB}{RS} = \frac{BC}{ST}$$

$$\frac{s}{5} = \frac{30}{6}$$

$$s \times 6 = 30 \times 5$$

$$6s = 150$$

$$\frac{6s}{6} = \frac{150}{6}$$

$$s = 25$$

Answer: The length of side *AB* is 25 feet.

Quiz

1. What is "2 more than the quotient of 5 and *k*" written as an algebraic expression?
   a. $2 + \frac{k}{5}$
   b. $2 \times \frac{5}{k}$
   c. $\frac{5}{k} + 2$
   d. $\frac{2+5}{k}$
   e. $\frac{2 \times 5}{k}$

2. What is the value of $18 + 3s$ when $s = 6$?
   a. 27
   b. 36
   c. 54
   d. 108
   e. 126

3. Simplify: $7x + y - 2x - y$
   a. $5x$
   b. $9x$
   c. $5x + 2y$
   d. $9x - 2y$
   e. $9xy - 3xy$

4. What is "5 less than the product of 8 and *y* is 12" written as an algebraic equation?
   a. $8y - 5 = 12$
   b. $5 - 8y = 12$
   c. $5 - 8 + y = 12$
   d. $5 - (8 + y) = 12$
   e. $(8 + y) - 5 = 12$

5. Solve: $2x - 7 + x = 38$
   a. $x = 10$
   b. $x = 15$
   c. $x = 28$
   d. $x = 31$
   e. $x = 45$

6. Which is the graph of $y = 3x - 4$?

a.

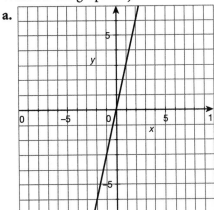

b.

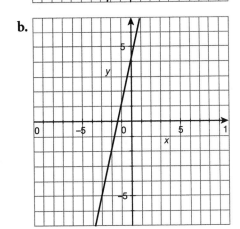

c.

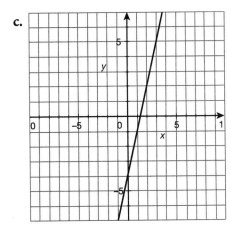

d.

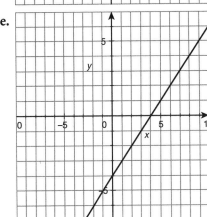

e.

7. The formula for the area of a triangle is $A = \frac{1}{2}bh$, where b = base and h = height. If the area of a triangle is 16 in.^{2} and the base is 4 in., what is h, the height of the triangle?

  a. $h = 4$ in.

  b. $h = 8$ in.

  c. $h = 12$ in.

  d. $h = 24$ in.

  e. $h = 32$ in.

8. A watermelon costs $1.50 per pound. How much would it cost if it weighs 3 pounds?

  a. $2.50

  b. $3.00

  c. $3.50

  d. $4.00

  e. $4.50

9. The scale on a map is 1 inch:10 miles. The distance between Point *X* and Point *Y* on the map is 3.5 inches. What is the actual distance between Point *X* and Point *Y*?

a. 0.35 miles

b. 13.5 miles

c. 35.0 miles

d. 135 miles

e. 350 miles

10. Trapezoid *KLMN* and trapezoid *OPQR* are similar.

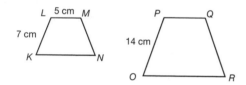

What is the length of side *PQ*?

a. 10 cm

b. 10.5 cm

c. 11 cm

d. 11.5 cm

e. 12 cm

Quiz Answers

1. c. The phrase "2 more than" means that 2 is added. This eliminates choices **b** and **e**, in which 2 is multiplied. The term "quotient" means to divide 5 by *k*, and while choice **a** is close, it reverses the terms. The correct expression is $\frac{5}{k} + 2$.

2. b. Since you have an equation, place the value of *s* as 6 into this equation and then solve.

$18 + 3s =$

$18 + 3(6) =$

$18 + 18 = 36$

So, $18 + 3s = 36$ when $s = 6$.

3. a. This is an algebraic expression, not an equation, so there is nothing to solve. You can, however, simplify by combining like terms. You have one positive *y* and one negative *y*, so these cancel each other out, just like 1 and −1 cancel each other out. There are also *x*'s, namely a 7*x* and a 2*x*, but pay attention to the subtraction sign in front of the 2*x*. This means that when these like terms are combined, the result is 5*x* (7 − 2), not 9*x* (7 + 2). The simplified expression is 5*x*.

4. a. The last part, "is 12," can be written mathematically as "= 12." Unfortunately, all answer choices have this at the end, so it does not help. The phrase "product" means to multiply, so 8 and *y* need to be multiplied. (Recalling order of operations, this must be done before addition/subtraction.) Then, "5 less" can be taken, or subtracted, from that product. The final algebraic equation would be $8y − 5 = 12$.

5. b. For a given equation, you can solve for x by getting x on one side of the equation and all the numerical values on the other.

$$2x - 7 + x = 38$$
$$2x + x - 7 = 38$$
$$3x - 7 = 38$$
$$3x - 7 + 7 = 38 + 7$$
$$3x = 45$$
$$\frac{3x}{3} = \frac{45}{3}$$
$$x = 15$$

6. c. To determine the correct graph, you need to find some coordinate values that fit into the equation $y = 3x - 4$. Look at how some graphs pass through the origin $(0,0)$, while others do not. What happens when you set x equal to zero and place it into the equation $y = 3x - 4$?

$$y = 3x - 4$$
$$y = 3(0) - 4$$
$$y = -4$$

This gives you the point $(0,-4)$. Only two graphs, choices **c** and **e**, pass through this point. If you set y equal to zero, then you get:

$$y = 3x - 4$$
$$0 = 3x - 4$$
$$4 + 0 = 3x - 4 + 4$$
$$4 = 3x$$
$$\frac{4}{3} = \frac{3x}{3}$$
$$\frac{4}{3} = x$$

Point $(4/3,0)$ or $(1.333,0)$ corresponds to graph **c**, not **e**.

7. b. In some ways this question is similar to Question 5, even if it does not appear so at first glance because of all the additional text. However, your goal is the same; set up an equation and then solve for the unknown variable.

$$A = \frac{1}{2}bh$$
$$16 = \frac{1}{2}(4)h$$
$$16 = 2h$$
$$\frac{16}{2} = \frac{2h}{2}$$
$$8 = h$$

The height of the triangle is 8 in.

8. e. Setting up a ratio can solve this problem, but you can also see that if the price of one pound of watermelon costs \$1.50, then three pounds will cost three times as much, or $(\$1.50)(3) = \$4.50$.

9. c. Here is another ratio problem, and although we could solve it like we did Question 8, we'll show the other approach. Set up a ratio, then cross-multiply.

$$\frac{1}{10} = \frac{3.5}{x}$$
$$(1)(x) = (3.5)(10)$$
$$x = 35$$

The actual distance between Point X and Point Y is 35 miles.

10. a. Since the trapezoids are similar, the ratios between their sides are also similar. This allows you to set up a ratio and then solve for side PQ.

$$\frac{LK}{LM} = \frac{PO}{PQ}$$
$$\frac{7}{5} = \frac{14}{PQ}$$
$$(7)(PQ) = (5)(14)$$
$$(7)(PQ) = 70$$
$$\frac{(7)(PQ)}{7} = \frac{70}{7}$$
$$PQ = 10$$

Side PQ is 10 cm long.

Algebraic Expressions

An algebraic expression has numbers, variables, and operation signs. We can simplify algebraic expressions by combining like terms and using the Distributive Property.

Algebraic Equations

An algebraic equation has numbers, variables, operation signs, and an equal sign. We use inverse operations and the Properties of Equality to solve for the variable(s) in the equation.

Equation of a Line

A line on a coordinate plane can be represented by an algebraic equation. If we know the equation of the line, we can create a table to find the x-coordinates and y-coordinates of various points on the line.

Formulas

A formula is an algebraic equation with variables on both sides of the equal sign. If the variable we want to solve for is on the side with the algebraic expression, we use inverse operations and the Properties of Equality to isolate it.

Proportions

We set up proportions to solve problems involving rates, scale drawings, and similar polygons. To solve a proportion, we cross multiply. Then we use the inverse of multiplication and the Division Property of Equality to isolate and solve for the variable.

TIPS AND STRATEGIES

CHAPTER SUMMARY

This chapter covers GED® test strategies. You'll learn how to tackle the different kinds of problems and sections found on the GED® Math exam. This chapter also outlines what you need to know before *and* during the test to succeed.

Congratulations! By going through the information in this book, you are already on the right track for doing your best on the GED® Math exam. There are a few other ways to make sure you are ready for the big day.

- **Remember that practice makes perfect.** Answer the practice questions in this book in the weeks and months before the test. Not only will you become more familiar and comfortable with the types of questions, but you'll also learn what skills you need to review.
- **Study ahead of time.** Cramming in the few days before the test is not the most effective way to study. Leave these last few days for a quick review.
- **Take a break.** Spend the day before the test doing something you enjoy. Watch a video, go for a jog, or hang out with friends. Get your mind off of math and relax.

■ **Gather your testing items.** Have your pencils, sweater, watch, water bottle, and anything else you plan to take to the test ready ahead of time.

■ **Get some sleep.** Go to bed early the night before the test so you're bright eyed and bushy tailed in the morning. If you're afraid you won't be able to go to sleep before your regular bedtime, get up early the morning before.

As you worked through this book, you reviewed a lot of skills that you will be expected to understand for the GED® Math exam. In this chapter, we'll go over a few general tips for doing your best on the test, as well as some things to keep in mind as you prepare for and answer each type of question.

You're probably thinking, "All of this is great, but how many questions do I have to get right to pass the test?" You will need to correctly answer approximately 60%–65% of the questions. This chapter will help you make the most of what you've learned throughout the book so you can do your best on the big day.

On the day of the test, you will be given two useful tools that will help you do your best. The first is a calculator, which you can use on Part I only; the second is a math formulas page.

GED® Strategies

There are a total of 50 questions on the GED® Math Test. These will be divided evenly between two 45-minute sessions. The two parts of the test will be evenly weighted when scored, but you will notice one major difference between them. On Part I of the test, you will be permitted to use a Casio fx-260 calculator, which will be provided by the testing center. However, you will not be allowed to use the calculator on Part II of the test.

After you finish Part I, you will turn in your test booklet and the calculator. Estimation and mental math are assessed on Part II of the test, so no calculator is allowed. If you finish Part II and still have time remaining, you can turn in the test booklet and get the calculator and the Part I booklet back to finish that section or check your work. However, once you have had the calculator again, you will not be allowed to return to Part II of the test. Make sure you have completely finished Part II and checked your work completely before returning to Part I.

Math Formulas Page

A page of math formulas will be provided for you to use as a reference during the entire test. The formulas listed on the page include:

- area of a square
- area of a rectangle
- area of a parallelogram
- area of a triangle
- area of a trapezoid
- area of a circle
- perimeter of a square
- perimeter of a rectangle
- perimeter of a triangle
- circumference of a circle
- volume of a cube
- volume of a rectangular solid

- volume of a square pyramid
- volume of a cylinder
- volume of a cone
- distance between points
- slope of a line
- Pythagorean relationship
- mean
- median
- simple interest
- distance
- total cost

Be sure you are familiar with each of the formulas before the test. While this page could definitely be helpful, it is up to you to know when to use each formula. For instance, suppose you need to find the area of a circle. On the formula page you will see:

Area of a circle
Area = $\pi \times radius^2$; π is approximately equal
   to 3.14

Being reminded of the formula is great, and could be very helpful if you sometimes confuse the formulas for area and circumference. But, unless you know what *radius* means, and how to find the square of its value, the formula won't do you much good.

Make sure you are familiar with shapes and the different types of graphs. If you are given a picture of a three-dimensional figure, but aren't sure whether you are looking at a rectangular solid or a square pyramid, you won't know which formula to use when calculating its volume.

Words such as *base, diameter, edge, hypotenuse, radius,* and *principal* are used on the formulas page, but are not defined. Make sure you know what each of these words means.

Types of Questions

The GED® Math Test has 50 questions, divided between two equally weighted sections. Part I and Part II of the test each contain 25 questions, and you will have 45 minutes to complete each part of the test.

The problems on each part of the test will be presented in the context of real-life situations and will measure your problem-solving abilities, as well as your analytical and reasoning skills. You will be expected to interpret information presented in word problems as well as in graphic displays such as tables, charts, graphs, and diagrams.

The test questions come from four basic areas of math:

- Number operations and number sense
- Measurement and geometry
- Data analysis, statistics, and probability
- Algebra, functions, and patterns

Each of these content areas will be represented by about 20%–30% of the questions on the test, and you will need to demonstrate the use of high-order thinking skills as you solve the problems. Let's talk about some tips for each of these content areas.

Number Operations and Number Sense

Number operations and number sense questions will be found on both Parts I and II of the GED® Math exam. For some, you will be able to use a calculator, but for others, you will not. Earlier in this book, you reviewed the skills needed to successfully answer these types of questions. Keep in mind that somewhere around one-fourth of the questions will relate to this content area.

Work Carefully
It is easy to make simple mistakes when you're stressed or feel rushed. Be sure to work carefully. Many mistakes that are made on this type of question are usually the result of careless errors in calculation. Don't miss a question that you know because of a misplaced decimal or a forgotten negative sign.

Practice Calculating Percentages
You already know that finding a percentage is as simple as dividing the numerator by the denominator. It can be easy to reverse these values during the test. Practice calculating percentages ahead of time, then checking to see if the result is reasonable. For example,

find the percentage of students on the football team who are juniors. If you determine that 3% of the players are in that class, you may want to double check your answer. Also, if you find that 125% of the players are juniors, you should be able to recognize that this is not a reasonable answer either.

Learn Benchmarks

Review benchmark square numbers in order to estimate the reasonableness of answers involving squares and square roots. If you know that:

- $10^2 = 100$
- $15^2 = 225$, and
- $20^2 = 400$,

you have a starting point for deciding if your answer on the test is feasible. Take a few minutes to calculate several other squares, and review these between now and test day.

Draw a Picture

Drawing a simple picture can help you visualize a problem. It can also help you see if your answer is reasonable.

Understand Exponents

Remember that exponents are not factors.

6^2 means 6×6, not 6×2.

Confusing the meaning of an exponent is a common mistake made on the GED® Math exam.

- base
- exponent
- integer
- prime number
- proportion
- rational number
- root
- scientific form

Round Fractions to Estimate

It can be helpful to round a fraction to the nearest whole number when deciding which operation to use to solve a problem. This allows you to see how the problem should be solved and how to find a reasonable answer. Check out this example.

$$3\tfrac{7}{8} + 5\tfrac{1}{9} =$$

Before you add these mixed numbers, round them to the nearest whole number.

$$4 + 5 =$$

Now you can estimate that when you add the fractions, the sum should be about 9, because $4 + 5 = 9$. You can easily tell if your answer is reasonable, or if you should try the problem again.

Convert Ratios to Decimals

Using a calculator to convert ratios to decimals can make it easier to compare the ratios. It can also save you some time, which is definitely a plus! Make sure you have written the ratio in its lowest terms before selecting the correct answer choice.

Review the Terms

Make sure you know the meanings of mathematical terms that are likely to show up in questions relating to number operations and number sense. Write the words and their meanings on flash cards or a study sheet and become familiar with them before the test.

Measurement and Geometry

Questions relating to measurement and geometry will also represent about 20%–30% of the items on the GED® Math exam and will be found on both Parts I and II. Keep these ideas in mind as you work through the practice questions, as well as the questions on the actual test.

Make It Simple

You will need to be able to find the area of an irregular figure. In other words, you will be given a figure that is not a simple rectangle. Don't let this confuse you. Divide the figure into smaller, simple shapes, and find the areas of each of the smaller sections. Then, add to find the total. For example, to find the area of an L-shaped vegetable garden, divide the garden into two smaller rectangles. Just make sure that you include every part of the irregular shape, and that each part is only included once.

TIP

You could put this strategy to use throughout the test, not just for geometry questions. Separate the more difficult problems into smaller, easier parts. Break questions down into pieces you can easily solve.

Look for Clues

Try to find clues that will help you figure out which formula to use to solve a problem. For example, if a question mentions putting a fence around the backyard, you can figure out that a fence goes around something, so you may need to find the perimeter. If you are asked to find how much paint a certain can holds, you know that volume tells how much something holds, so you'll probably need the formula for volume.

Shape Up

Some problems that involve geometric figures may not include a picture of the shape. If this happens, make a drawing of the shape described. Label the shape with any information given, such as measurements or angle names. Being able to visualize the problem can help you find the correct answer more easily.

Review the Terms

You will find quite a few measurement and geometry terms on the test. It will be important that you know the meanings of each in order to correctly answer the questions. Some words to review are listed on the following page.

- point
- ray
- line
- line segment
- intersect
- acute angle
- obtuse angle
- right angle
- reflex angles
- supplementary angles
- complementary angles
- adjacent angles
- vertical angles
- quadrilateral

- rectangle
- square
- rhombus
- parallelogram
- trapezoid
- radius
- circumference
- diameter
- perimeter
- cube
- face
- rectangular solid
- square pyramid
- cylinder

- vertex
- cone
- sphere
- equilateral triangle
- isosceles triangle
- scalene triangle
- right triangle
- hypotenuse
- perpendicular
- parallel
- congruent
- similar
- translation
- rotation

Data Analysis, Statistics, and Probability

Although graphic displays of information will be used in each of the content areas, you can expect to find quite a few graphs, tables, and charts in questions that relate to data analysis, statistics, and probability.

Read All About It

Be sure to read all titles, labels, keys, and other information included with graphs and tables. This information could make a big difference in how you interpret the data. For example, if a graph or table includes a label that reads *Cost in Hundreds of Dollars*, the graph itself could show 25; however, data should be interpreted to mean $2,500.

See the Data

When asked to select the correct data display based on information given in the text, try to visualize the situation that has been described. Then try drawing your own simple graph. This can be helpful in choosing the graph that correctly shows the information.

Sometimes use scratch paper...

To find the median of a set of data, write the values in ascending order on a piece of scratch paper first. It is much easier to find the number whose value is in the middle of the set if the values are in order.

> Writing the values in order can also be helpful when determining the mode. By doing this, you are less likely to overlook or miscount how many times a value appears in the set.

...and other times use a calculator.

If the calculator is available, use it to quickly determine the mean of a set of data. This may be a skill that you are comfortable doing on paper, but using the calculator will save valuable time.

Review the Terms

Be sure you understand the difference between the measures of central tendency of a data set.

- mean
- median
- mode

Algebra, Functions, and Patterns

Many questions relating to algebra, functions, and patterns will include variables, expressions, and graphs. As with the other content areas, these types of questions will make up 20%–30% of the test.

Understand the Unknown

Some people get nervous when they see letters in the middle of math problems. Don't let that happen to you. Remember that a variable is simply an unknown number.

Also, when you write a word problem as an algebraic expression, substitute a variable for the unknown value. Keep in mind that a variable does not have to be x or y. Choose a variable that makes sense to you. For example, use m to represent an unknown number of miles, or k to represent Kate's age.

- absolute value
- expression
- inequality
- variable

- origin
- positive slope
- negative slope

Look at the Problems in a New Way

If you are not sure of how to solve a problem, look for ways to use formulas you already know. For example, the Pythagorean Theorem may be helpful in solving problems that at first do not appear to have a right triangle. Draw an equilateral or isosceles triangle. A line drawn down the middle to find the height also creates two identical right triangles. Given the correct information, it could be possible to use the theorem to find the sides of the original triangle.

Read the Whole Problem

Always read the entire word problem before writing an equation or inequality to solve it. Sometimes important information is presented at the end.

Review the terms...

Some of the words you can expect to find in questions related to algebra, functions, and patterns are listed here. Being completely sure of their meanings will help you feel more comfortable and confident on test day.

- zero slope
- undefined slope
- intercept

TIP

If you make flash cards or a study sheet to practice these terms, consider including a drawing as well as a definition when applicable. For example, reading the definition of a positive slope, then seeing an example of one on a graph, can make the term more meaningful.

...and the symbols.

In addition to knowing the meanings of the words above, make sure you also recognize and know the meanings of these inequality symbols:

$$< \qquad > \qquad \leq \qquad \geq$$

Using the Calculator

You have probably used a calculator many times in the past. A few simple reminders can help you make the most of this tool on the GED® Math Test. Directions for using the calculator you will be given can be found in the test booklet for Part I. Make sure to look over these directions on the day of the test.

Start with a Clean Slate

Always hit the AC button on the calculator before every question to make sure the memory is completely clear. Having numbers left in the calculator from a previous question can cause you to get the wrong answer.

Repeat Yourself

Do all calculator problems twice just in case you incorrectly entered a value or hit the wrong operator. If you get the same answer twice, great! If not, try again.

Practice

Practice using the calculator. Put in simple problems that you know the answers to, just to be sure you are inputting them correctly.

In the past, you have probably used calculators to perform basic operations. But have you used a calculator to solve expressions with exponents or square roots?

How to Solve Exponents

To square a number, use the x^2 key. To find 15^2, press the following buttons on the calculator:

1. AC
2. 1
3. 5
4. x^2

To find the cube of a number, you use the x^y key. To find 5^3, press:

1. AC
2. 5
3. x^y
4. 3

To raise a number to a higher power, follow the same steps. Just press the exponent you need after the x^y key.

How to Find Square Roots

To find a square root, use the $\sqrt{}$ key. First, enter the number, then press the square root key. For example, to find the square root of 25, press:

1. 25
2. $\sqrt{}$

Push the Right Buttons

The calculator you will be provided already has the order of operations programmed into it. Input the numbers and symbols exactly as they appear in the problem. A few other things to keep in mind are listed next:

- Remember to press the multiplication button before hitting the parentheses key. For example, the expression $3(6-2)$ would need a multiplication symbol entered right after the 3.
- Make sure to include decimal points. Leaving out a decimal point can completely change your answer.
- Press the equal sign after entering arithmetic problems. Otherwise, the last operation entered might not have been applied yet.
- Use the +/− key to create negative numbers.

Graphics

Many items on the test involve some sort of graphic. These questions must be answered based on information provided in the test, the visual aid, or both.

Read Carefully

Carefully read the information in the question. You may need to use information from a graph or table to calculate the correct answer. Be careful not to simply choose the data from the table and assume that the information stated is the correct answer. You may have to do something with the data in order to find the answer.

Become Familiar with Data Displays

Practice writing your own questions based on tables and graphs found in newspapers or textbooks. As you look at the graphic, think about what it is showing and how this information looks in a visual display.

Also, practice making your own graphs to become more comfortable with visual displays. For example, graph the high temperature in your city over a period of several days. Use a different color to graph the high temperature in a city you have visited, and compare the data.

Calculate the Answers

Visual aids such as diagrams, maps, and geometric shapes may or may not be drawn to scale on the test. Do not choose an answer based on how a graphic looks. Take the time to do the math.

Solving Word Problems

As you already know, the questions on the GED® Math Test are presented in real-life contexts. In other words, they are word problems. As you work, keep these few hints in mind.

Read Carefully

Read the question carefully and be sure you understand exactly what it is asking, and what type of answer is needed. For example, do you need to find the distance someone traveled, how many miles per hour they traveled, or how many hours it took to get there? Pay attention to details. Underline or circle key information.

Choose the Important Information

Determine what information you need to answer the question. Nonessential information may be included. Ignore or cross off that information.

Estimate

Estimate, then find the answer. Think about what size or type of answer makes sense. Later, you can use the estimate to determine whether or not your answer is reasonable. For example, if you are calculating sales tax, you can estimate that the correct answer will probably be less than 10%. If you find an answer that is significantly higher than your estimate, you'll know it would be a good idea to try solving the problem again.

Look for Key Words

Often, key words will give hints about what operations are needed to solve a problem. For example, *all together* is often a clue that you should add. Keep your eye out for words such as these:

- in all
- total
- difference
- less than

- sum
- product
- quotient
- per

- ratio
- increase

Take All the Right Steps

Ask yourself if more than one step is needed to solve the problem. There are times that two or more steps may be needed, such as adding and then dividing to find the mean. Make sure that you completely solve the problem; your solution should make sense as the answer to the original question.

Even if you perform only some of the steps in a solution, your answer may be one of the choices. Be careful to completely solve the problem before selecting your answer.

Check Your Work

Always check your work. Is your answer close to your estimate? If so, great! Make sure the answer you found is right. You might do this by adding to check subtraction, or multiplying to check division, for example. You might also reread the problem and look for another way to solve it. See if you get the same answer again. Make sure the answer you found is one of the answer choices on multiple choice questions. If it isn't, you know you'll need to do something differently.

TIP

Write down the solution to each step as you solve the problems. This will make it easier to see where you may have made a mistake if you need to correct an answer.

Question Yourself

Ask yourself if your answer makes sense in the context of the question. If you determine that a high school student makes $132 per hour working at a fast-food restaurant, you should probably recheck your work.

Answering Multiple Choice Questions

Eighty percent of the questions on the GED® Math Test, will be **multiple choice**. The remaining 20% will be **alternate format questions**, in which you will have to construct your own response and record it on either a standard grid or a coordinate plane grid. You will find all of these types of questions on both Parts I and II of the test.

Some groups of questions will be in **question sets**. That means between 2 and 4 questions will be asked about the same information, such as a paragraph or visual aid.

Choose the BEST Answer

The key to doing well on multiple-choice questions is to select the *best* answer. You may find that more than one option looks tempting. There's a reason for that. While there is only one best answer for each question, the incorrect answer choices are based on common mistakes that students make. It is definitely possible for your wrong answer to be one of the choices listed. Just because you see your first answer listed, that does not mean that it is the correct answer or the best choice.

Answer Every Question

Any question you leave blank is marked wrong, so you want to be sure you have an answer for every question. You may come across a problem that you just aren't sure about. Make sure you at least take your best guess and choose an answer.

Eliminate Incorrect Choices

Before you guess, it is important to eliminate as many of the wrong answer choices as possible. The more choices you are able to eliminate, the better your chances of selecting the correct answer.

Randomly guessing gives you a 1 in 5 chance of choosing the right answer. If you can eliminate even one incorrect choice, your chances improve. If you can eliminate three choices, you have improved the odds significantly—you'd have a fifty-fifty chance of getting the answer right!

Here are a few ideas to help you figure out which incorrect choices to eliminate:

- **Use logic.** Suppose you have determined that the answer has to be negative; now you can eliminate any positive answers. Or, if you are multiplying fractions, you know that the answer must be a smaller fraction, and any larger answer choices are not correct.
- **Estimate.** Estimate what the correct answer should be, and look for an answer choice that is close to that value. Or at least eliminate choices that are too far off from the estimate. For example, if you look at a circle graph and need to find the percentage represented by a section that is slightly less than one quarter of the graph, you could reasonable exclude any answer that would indicate more than 25%.
- **Look for extremes.** If an answer stands out as being very different from the rest, you might consider eliminating this choice. For example, if four answer choices are whole numbers and one is a decimal, it is not likely that the decimal is the correct answer.

Substitute

Try substituting each answer choice into the problem and see if it works. For example, if you are trying to find the value of the variable in $3x + 7 = 40$, you can replace the variable with each of the answer choices and solve the equation to find which choice is correct.

Answering Alternate-Format Questions

One-fifth of the items on the test will require you to come up with the answer, then record it on a grid. In other words, you will not have answer choices to choose from. You'll have to find an answer on your own.

Gridded Response Items

To record answers to these questions, you will write each digit, decimal point, or fraction bar in boxes on the top row of a grid. In the column beneath each number or symbol, you will fill in the bubble that represents that character. Any unused columns will be left blank.

For example, an answer of 34.4 would look like this:

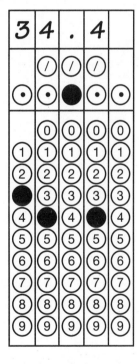

As you work, keep these tips in mind:

- **All of the answers will be positive.** If you come up with an answer that is a negative number, you've made a mistake. Try the problem again.
- **Mixed numbers cannot be entered into the grid.** These must be shown as decimals or fractions. So, if the answer is $3\frac{1}{2}$, you must grid either 3.5 or $\frac{7}{2}$ as your answer.

You will use a slash (/) for the fraction bar in gridded response items. It is located in the top row of the grid, just below the blank boxes where you write the characters.

Timing Is Everything

You will have 45 minutes to answer the 25 questions on each part of the GED® Math exam; that's a total of 90 minutes to answer all 50 questions. It will be important for you to be aware of how much time has passed and how long you have left to finish the test.

Pace Yourself

Ninety minutes may sound like a long time, but there will be less than two minutes to answer each question. Aim for spending about one and a half minutes or less on each question. That way, you'll have a little bit of time to spare if you get stuck on a question, and you'll have time to go over your answers at the end of the test.

To make sure you have plenty of time to finish each part of the test, try to answer:

- 10 questions in the first 15 minutes
- 20 questions in the first 30 minutes
- 25 questions by the end of 38 minutes

This plan leaves 7 minutes to check your work once you've finished. It also gives you a little wiggle room if you find a question or two that are especially tricky and take a few extra seconds.

It is important to work quickly, but more importantly, to work carefully. If you rush, it is more likely that you'll make mistakes. Keep the time limit in the back of your mind and focus on doing your best!

Keep an Eye on the Time

Make sure you wear a watch on test day. Be aware of what time each section of the test begins, and figure out what time the section will end. The test administrator will probably let you know how much time you have left, but it would be good to monitor this yourself. That way, if you find you are ahead of schedule, you can relax a bit. If questions are taking longer than planned, you can try to work a little faster.

Coordinate Plane Grids

To record an answer on these grids, you will find the point located at the correct coordinates, then fill in the bubble at that location on the grid.

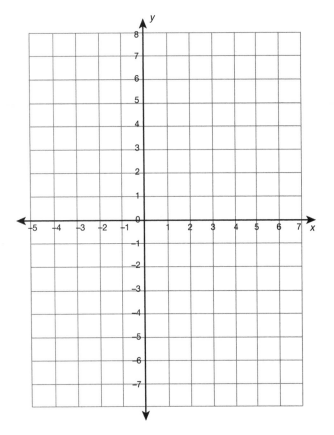

- **Answers must have both x- and y-values.** Make sure you find an answer that has both.
- **Answers will only be whole numbers.** No value on the grid will be a fraction or a decimal.
- **Answers can be positive or negative.** Mark your choices carefully on the grid.

Keep in mind that you may not be allowed to wear a watch that has a calculator. Choose a different timepiece for test day.

Make the Most of Your Time

Remember, you are trying to spend only about a minute and a half on each question. If you are having trouble finding a specific answer, take your best guess and move on to the next question. Spending too much time on one difficult question can cause you to run out of the time to solve other problems that you think are a snap.

If you have extra time, you can always come back later and take another stab at that tricky question. You might even think the question is easier the second time around.

Beat the Clock

You've paced yourself, kept an eye on the clock, and used your time wisely. So what happens if time is almost up and you're still not finished? Start guessing. You already know that any answer that is left blank will be marked wrong. Use the last couple of minutes to quickly mark an answer for every item. You may not get them all right, but at least you have a chance of racking up a few extra correct answers.

Test Day

Finally, the big day is here! You've studied, you've practiced, and now you are ready to do your best!

Before you leave the house...

- **Give yourself some time.** Make sure your clock is set early enough that you'll be able to get ready without having to rush. Try to start the day relaxed and without getting stressed about being on time. Keep in mind that some testing centers may not allow people to come in if they are late.

- **Eat a good breakfast.** You already know that breakfast is the most important meal of the day. Starting the morning with a well-balanced meal will not only help you keep your energy up, but will also help you focus on something other than your stomach. If nerves are getting the best of you, at least grab some trail mix, a piece of fruit, or some toast and juice. You might also want to bring a snack if you have a long day of testing scheduled.

- **Be comfortable.** Choose clothes that are comfortable and help you feel confident. Dressing in layers and bringing a light sweater or jacket will be helpful if the testing room is not the perfect temperature. You want to focus on the test, not on being too cold.

During the Test

It's finally here. The test is in front of you, and it is time to begin. Take a deep breath and remember exactly what this is. It is JUST a test. Of course you want to get every single question right, but the world will not come to an end if things don't go as well as you planned. If necessary, you can take the test up to three times in a calendar year. Just stay focused, do your best, and be confident in knowing that you are as ready as you can be.

Read Everything Carefully

Look over the directions for using the calculator, locate the formulas page, and read the questions and their directions very carefully. If anything is unclear, ask the test administrator. He or she can't help you with specific problems on the test but may be able to clarify the instructions.

Mark Your Answers Clearly and Completely

Remember that the test is checked by a computer. It is important to completely fill in each answer bubble you choose. Be careful not to make any stray marks on the answer sheet, and completely erase any answers that you change. Also make sure that only a single answer is marked for each question. Any item that has two answers filled in will be marked wrong.

Keep Your Place

Make sure you mark each multiple-choice answer in the corresponding place on the answer sheet. In other words, make sure your answer to question 1 is marked next to the number 1 on the answer sheet. This is especially important to remember if you decide to skip any questions.

A Final Word

Give yourself a pat on the back! You are taking charge of your own learning and preparing for a big step into your future. Knowing what to expect and being prepared are great tools to take with you into the GED® Math exam.

Throughout this book, you have reviewed quite a few math skills, gone over a number of mathematical vocabulary words, and been given several test-taking tips that will help you do your best, not only on this math test, but also on any math test that you encounter. Now, answer the practice questions, brush up on any skills you find challenging, and keep the tips you have learned in mind. You are well on your way to a great experience with the GED® Math exam. Best of luck!

PRACTICE TEST 1

This is the first of two practice tests based on the GED® Math Test. After working through the review in Chapters 3–7, take this test to see how much your score has improved from the Diagnostic Test.

You are now familiar with the kinds of questions and answer formats you will see on the official GED® Test. Now take this posttest to identify any areas that you may need to review in more depth before the test day. When you are finished, check the answers on page 148 carefully to assess your results.

Remember to:

- Work carefully
- Use estimation to eliminate answer choices or to check your work
- Answer every question
- Check to make sure your answers are logical
- Use the formula cheat sheet on pages 181 and 182, when needed

To simulate the test conditions, use the time constraints of the official GED® Mathematics Test. Allow 45 minutes for Part I. You may use a calculator to answer these 25 questions. Then, give yourself 45 minutes for Part II. You should not use a calculator for these 25 questions.

Remember, on the official GED® Test, an unanswered question is counted as incorrect, so make a good guess on questions you're not sure about.

Directions: Read each of the questions that follow carefully and determine the best answer. Record your answers by filling in the circles on the answer sheet provided for multiple-choice and alternative-format questions.

Note: On the GED® Test, you are not permitted to write in the test booklet. For this pretest, practice by making any notes or calculations on a separate piece of paper.

Part I

1.	ⓐ	ⓑ	ⓒ	ⓓ	ⓔ	**10.**	ⓐ	ⓑ	ⓒ	ⓓ	ⓔ	**19.**	ⓐ	ⓑ	ⓒ	ⓓ	ⓔ
2.	ⓐ	ⓑ	ⓒ	ⓓ	ⓔ	**11.**	ⓐ	ⓑ	ⓒ	ⓓ	ⓔ	**20.**	ⓐ	ⓑ	ⓒ	ⓓ	ⓔ
3.	ⓐ	ⓑ	ⓒ	ⓓ	ⓔ	**12.**	ⓐ	ⓑ	ⓒ	ⓓ	ⓔ	**21.**	ⓐ	ⓑ	ⓒ	ⓓ	ⓔ
4.	ⓐ	ⓑ	ⓒ	ⓓ	ⓔ	**13.**	ⓐ	ⓑ	ⓒ	ⓓ	ⓔ	**22.**	ⓐ	ⓑ	ⓒ	ⓓ	ⓔ
5.	ⓐ	ⓑ	ⓒ	ⓓ	ⓔ	**14.**	ⓐ	ⓑ	ⓒ	ⓓ	ⓔ	**23.**	ⓐ	ⓑ	ⓒ	ⓓ	ⓔ
6.	ⓐ	ⓑ	ⓒ	ⓓ	ⓔ	**15.**	ⓐ	ⓑ	ⓒ	ⓓ	ⓔ	**24.**	ⓐ	ⓑ	ⓒ	ⓓ	ⓔ
7.	ⓐ	ⓑ	ⓒ	ⓓ	ⓔ	**16.**	ⓐ	ⓑ	ⓒ	ⓓ	ⓔ	**25.**	ⓐ	ⓑ	ⓒ	ⓓ	ⓔ
8.	ⓐ	ⓑ	ⓒ	ⓓ	ⓔ	**17.**	ⓐ	ⓑ	ⓒ	ⓓ	ⓔ						
9.	ⓐ	ⓑ	ⓒ	ⓓ	ⓔ	**18.**	ⓐ	ⓑ	ⓒ	ⓓ	ⓔ						

Part II

1.	ⓐ	ⓑ	ⓒ	ⓓ	ⓔ	**10.**	ⓐ	ⓑ	ⓒ	ⓓ	ⓔ	**19.**	ⓐ	ⓑ	ⓒ	ⓓ	ⓔ
2.	ⓐ	ⓑ	ⓒ	ⓓ	ⓔ	**11.**	ⓐ	ⓑ	ⓒ	ⓓ	ⓔ	**20.**	ⓐ	ⓑ	ⓒ	ⓓ	ⓔ
3.	ⓐ	ⓑ	ⓒ	ⓓ	ⓔ	**12.**	ⓐ	ⓑ	ⓒ	ⓓ	ⓔ	**21.**	ⓐ	ⓑ	ⓒ	ⓓ	ⓔ
4.	ⓐ	ⓑ	ⓒ	ⓓ	ⓔ	**13.**	ⓐ	ⓑ	ⓒ	ⓓ	ⓔ	**22.**	ⓐ	ⓑ	ⓒ	ⓓ	ⓔ
5.	ⓐ	ⓑ	ⓒ	ⓓ	ⓔ	**14.**	ⓐ	ⓑ	ⓒ	ⓓ	ⓔ	**23.**	ⓐ	ⓑ	ⓒ	ⓓ	ⓔ
6.	ⓐ	ⓑ	ⓒ	ⓓ	ⓔ	**15.**	ⓐ	ⓑ	ⓒ	ⓓ	ⓔ	**24.**	ⓐ	ⓑ	ⓒ	ⓓ	ⓔ
7.	ⓐ	ⓑ	ⓒ	ⓓ	ⓔ	**16.**	ⓐ	ⓑ	ⓒ	ⓓ	ⓔ	**25.**	ⓐ	ⓑ	ⓒ	ⓓ	ⓔ
8.	ⓐ	ⓑ	ⓒ	ⓓ	ⓔ	**17.**	ⓐ	ⓑ	ⓒ	ⓓ	ⓔ						
9.	ⓐ	ⓑ	ⓒ	ⓓ	ⓔ	**18.**	ⓐ	ⓑ	ⓒ	ⓓ	ⓔ						

Part I—Calculator Allowed

You have 45 minutes to complete the following 25 questions.

1. John found that Nation B's outstanding national debt is approximately $14,000,000,000,000. Which is the correct scientific notation to express this figure?
   a. 1.4×10^{13}
   b. 1.4×10^{12}
   c. 14×10^{11}
   d. 14×10^{13}
   e. 14×10^{14}

Question 2 refers to the following diagram.

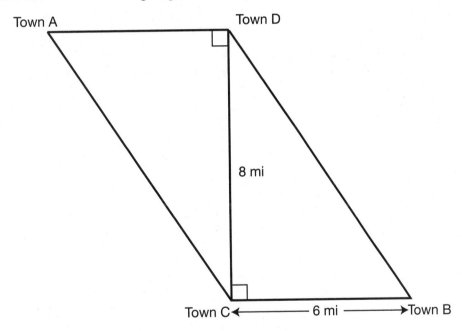

2. What is the distance between Town B and Town D?

   a. 0.1 mi
   b. 8 mi
   c. 10 mi
   d. 12 mi
   e. 14 mi

Questions 3 and 4 refer to the following diagram.

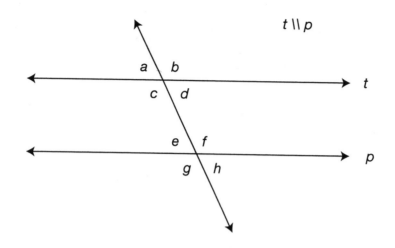

t \\ *p*

3. Which statement best accurately describes the angles in the diagram?
   a. ∠b and ∠d are congruent.
   b. ∠b and ∠h are congruent
   c. The sum of ∠e and ∠g is 180°.
   d. The sum of ∠f and ∠g is 180°.
   e. The sum of ∠e, ∠f, and ∠g is 180°.

4. If *m*∠e is 64°, what is the measurement of ∠d?
   a. 64°
   b. 116°
   c. 126°
   d. 180°
   e. 296°

Questions 5 through 7 refer to the following illustration.

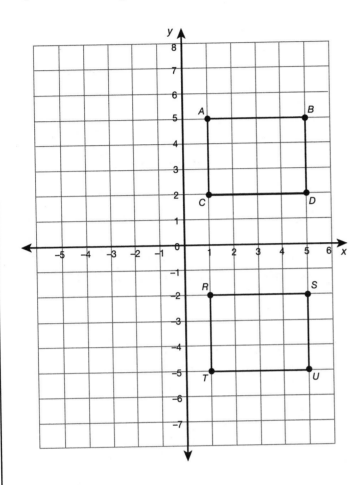

5. What is the area of rectangle ABDC?

   a. 6 units squared

   b. 12 units squared

   c. 18 units squared

   d. 24 units squared

   e. 36 units squared

6. Which line of reflection is used by rectangle ABDC to form rectangle RSUT?

   a. x-axis

   b. y-axis

   c. $x = 1$

   d. $y = 1$

   e. $y = -1$

7. Mark the coordinates of all four points that make up a new rectangle MNOP, which is a reflection of RSUT over the *y*-axis.

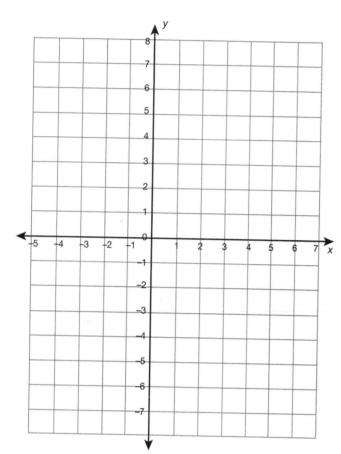

Question 9 refers to the following illustration.

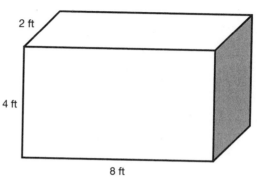

2 ft

4 ft

8 ft

9. Hallie has a storage space that has the dimensions of 2 feet by 4 feet by 8 feet. She now needs one that is double in volume. What is the volume, in cubic feet, of this new storage space?

Mark your answer in the grid on the answer sheet.

8. David is making a long-distance trip from Smithtown to Sayville, a town that is 500 miles away. Approximately how many miles per hour must he drive to reach his destination in 8 hours?

a. 40 miles per hour

b. 45 miles per hour

c. 50 miles per hour

d. 60 miles per hour

e. 70 miles per hour

10. Andrew is preparing to sell his baseball card collection at a backyard sale this weekend. He has 4,378 baseball cards in his collection. Rounded to the nearest hundred, how many baseball cards does he have?
    a. 4,000
    b. 4,300
    c. 4,370
    d. 4,380
    e. 4,400

11. Which number can be used to accurately express four million, two hundred forty thousand, five hundred seventeen?
    a. 4,002,417
    b. 4,204,517
    c. 4,240,517
    d. 4,247,017
    e. 4,427,517

12. Mr. Latif is making soup and salad for his dinner guests this evening. He bought $5\frac{1}{2}$ pounds of black beans and $6\frac{1}{4}$ pounds of green beans. How many pounds of beans did Mr. Latif purchase altogether? Mark your answer in the grid on the answer sheet.

13. Mr. Osaka is building a fence to protect his garden from animal intruders. He is fencing the garden, which is $12\frac{1}{2}$ feet wide and $16\frac{1}{8}$ feet long. How many feet of fencing will Mr. Osaka need to purchase?
    a. $57\frac{1}{4}$
    b. $57\frac{1}{2}$
    c. $58\frac{1}{10}$
    d. $38\frac{1}{5}$
    e. $38\frac{1}{2}$

Questions 14 and 15 refer to the following partial sales report.

Item ID	Item	Quantity	Unit Price	Amount
15-A155	MP3 Players	3		$375.75
74-B156	Laptops	2	$857.36	
14-C256	Flat Panel TV	2	$1,253.36	
			Total	

14. What is the total amount of sales for items 14-C256 and 74-B156?

a. $857.36

b. $1,127.25

c. $1,714.72

d. $2,506.72

e. $4,221.44

15. A correction on the sales report indicates that two additional Flat Panel TVs were sold. What is the total amount of TV sales with this correction?

a. $1,253.36

b. $2,506.72

c. $3,760.08

d. $4,221.44

e. $5,013.44

Question 16 refers to the following circle graph.

Dessert Preference Survey for Perkins High School

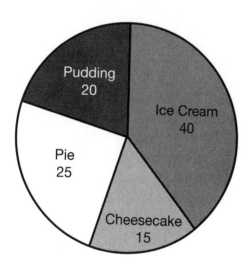

16. What is the ratio of students who prefer cheesecake to ice cream?

a. 40:15

b. 5:8

c. 3:8

d. 3:20

e. 5:3

17. To accelerate her university studies, Haley enrolled in an online course this term. She has completed 12.5% of her online course thus far. Which fraction of the course has Kathy completed?

Mark your answer in the grid on the answer sheet.

18. What is the value of the following expression?

$$125 + 20 \times 2 - (2 \times 12)$$

a. 109
b. 141
c. 150
d. 246
e. 266

Question 19 refers to the following information.

Super Office Store uses the following formula to determine how much to charge for each report photocopied.

Total Cost = c + 0.125p$ + $0.15

c = cost of cover illustration
p = number of pages
$0.15 is the binding fee, per report

19. John is preparing a 15-page presentation report for his company. The cover costs $0.15 per report. He needs to make 140 copies of this report for distribution. How much will it cost to print these reports?

Mark your answer in the grid on the answer sheet.

20. Which two values of x satisfy the equation $x^2 - 3x - 10 = 0$?

  a. {7,3}

  b. {−7,3}

  c. {7,−3}

  d. {5,2}

  e. {5,−2}

21. It was −2 degrees in Chicago this morning. The temperature has risen 8 degrees in the afternoon. What was the temperature in the afternoon?

  a. −10°

  b. −6°

  c. −4°

  d. 10°

  e. 6°

22. The Charging Raiders won 60% of their games last season. If each season has 80 games, how many games did the Charging Raiders lose last season?

  a. 32

  b. 45

  c. 48

  d. 133

  e. 155

23. Jack took out a $2,350 car loan for three years. If the interest rate is 6.25%, how much money will Jack have to pay back, including interest?

  a. 440.63

  b. 1,787.78

  c. 2,790.63

  d. 3,416.25

  e. 4,406.25

24. Which equation can be written as $y \div 16 = 4$?

  a. A number divided by sixteen equals four.

  b. Four divided by sixteen equals a number.

  c. A number divided by four equals sixteen.

  d. Four times sixteen equals a number.

  e. Sixteen times four equals a number.

Question 25 refers to the following coordinate plane grid.

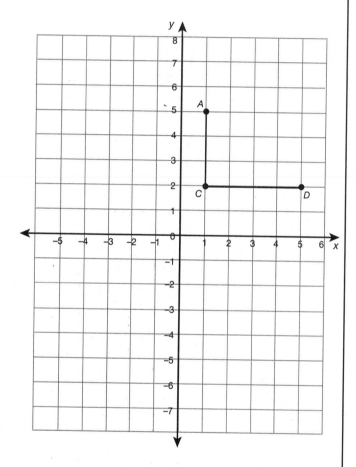

25. Mark the missing point of the coordinate plane grid that completes the rectangle ABDC.

STOP. DO NOT PROCEED TO THE NEXT SECTION UNTIL THE 45 MINUTES FOR PART I ARE COMPLETED.

Part II—NO Calculator

You have 45 minutes to complete the following 25 questions.

1. What is the slope of the line whose equation is $2x - 3y - 9 = 0$?

Mark your answer in the grid on the answer sheet.

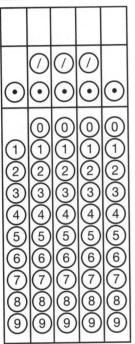

2. Adam is packing his luggage for his flight to San Francisco. The airport only allows luggage that weighs less than 50 pounds. Adam's suitcase is 87 pounds. Which expression can be used to find out how much weight Adam needs to remove from his luggage?

a. $w = 50 + 87$
b. $50 \div 87 = w$
c. $87 - 50 = w$
d. $w = (50 \times 87) + (87 - 50)$
e. $w = (87 \div 50) + 87$

3. John scores 117, 77, 198, 165, and 198 in a local bowling tournament. What is the median score for this tournament?

a. 77
b. 87
c. 151
d. 165
e. 198

Questions 4 and 5 refer to the following graph.

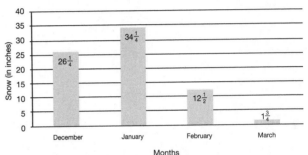

4. How many inches of snow had fallen in January and February?

a. $21\frac{1}{4}$
b. $21\frac{3}{4}$
c. $46\frac{1}{4}$
d. $46\frac{3}{4}$
e. $60\frac{1}{2}$

5. How many more inches of snow had fallen in January than in March?

a. 20
b. $20\frac{1}{4}$
c. $32\frac{1}{2}$
d. $32\frac{3}{4}$
e. 36

Question 6 refers to the following illustration.

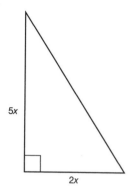

6. Which algebraic expression can be used to represent the area of this triangle?
   a. $10x^2$
   b. $5x^2$
   c. $\frac{1}{4}x^2$
   d. $2x^2$
   e. $10x$

7. Carmelo plans a hiking trip on a trail in a national park. The trail is 25 miles long. Which other information is necessary to find out the time it will take for Carmelo to finish this trail?
   a. The size of the park
   b. The rate of travel
   c. The starting time of the trip
   d. The weather conditions
   e. The perimeter of the park

8. Suppose these cards will be drawn at random. What is the probability of picking a nonwhite card?

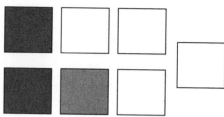

   a. $\frac{1}{7}$
   b. $\frac{2}{7}$
   c. $\frac{3}{7}$
   d. $\frac{4}{7}$
   e. $\frac{5}{7}$

9. The scale is 2 inches to 40 miles on a city map. The distance between Town A and Town B on the map is 5 inches. What is the actual distance in miles?
   a. 80 miles
   b. 40 miles
   c. 90 miles
   d. 100 miles
   e. 200 miles

10. Daquan receives $75 for a five-day football camp. The camp cafeteria charges x dollars for lunch each day. Which equation can best be used to represent the amount of money Daquan has left after paying for lunches during football camp?
   a. $m = \$75 - 5x$
   b. $m = \$75x$
   c. $m = 5x$
   d. $m = \$75 + 5x$
   e. $m = x - \$75x$

11. Which line is parallel to the line $y = \frac{1}{2}x + 8$?

    a. $y = 2x$

    b. $y = \frac{1}{2}x - 8$

    c. $y = -\frac{1}{2}x + 3$

    d. $y = 3x + 8$

    e. $y = 2x + 8$

12. Which value can be used for n in the following equation?

$$\frac{5}{6} = \frac{n}{12}$$

    a. 10

    b. 21

    c. 24

    d. 36

    e. 60

13. Anthony makes $1,500 per month. $195 was deducted for federal and state taxes. What percentage of Anthony's pay was deducted for taxation?

    a. 12%

    b. 13%

    c. 15%

    d. 16%

    e. 25%

14. A speaker system is discounted at 25% off the original price. If the original price is $234, what is the discounted price?

    a. $58.50

    b. $175.50

    c. $230

    d. $250

    e. $526.50

Questions 15 and 16 refer to the following line graph.

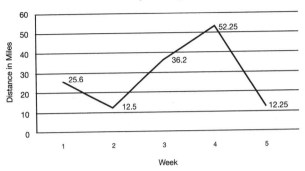

Johnny's Biking Training

15. How many miles did Johnny travel in weeks 3 through 5 combined?

    a. 74.3

    b. 88.45

    c. 100.7

    d. 164.4

    e. 328.8

16. How many more miles did Johnny travel during week 4 than during week 5?

    a. 13.1

    b. 16.05

    c. 23.7

    d. 40

    e. 64.5

17. Show the location of the *y*-intercept of the equation $y = 3x + 4$.

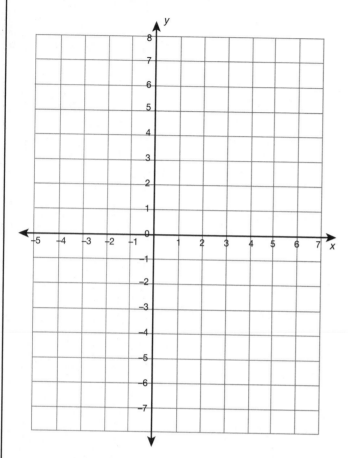

18. What is the distance from point *A* (−7,0) to point *B* (1,6)?

  a. 10
  b. 11
  c. 12
  d. 13
  e. 14

19. Dana bought 2 bags of lollipops for $2.25 each and 4 boxes of chocolate for $5.45 each. Which expression can best be used to determine the total amount Dana spent?

  a. $(2 \times \$2.25) + (4 \times \$5.45)$
  b. $(2 \times \$2.25) + (2 \times \$5.45)$
  c. $(6 \times \$2.25) + (6 \times \$5.45)$
  d. $\$2.25 \times \$2.25 + \$5.45$
  e. $\$2.25 \times \$5.45$

Question 20 refers to the following chart.

Joseph recorded his calorie intake for five days this week in the following chart.

Day	Calories
Monday	2,500
Tuesday	1,800
Wednesday	2,300
Thursday	2,300
Friday	1,700

20. What is the mode of this set of numbers?

  a. 2,500
  b. 1,800
  c. 1,900
  d. 2,300
  e. 1,700

21. Show the location of the point (−2,−5) on the coordinate plane grid.

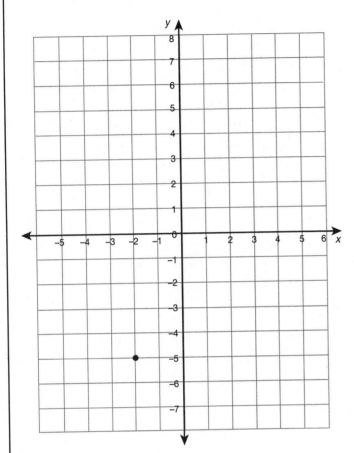

22. Which algebraic expression represents the product of $8m(2m − 1)$?
a. $16m^2 − 8m$
b. $2m^2 − 8m$
c. $8 − 16m^2$
d. $10m − 8$
e. $6m − 8$

23. Pedro is filling a tank with 3,000,000 milliliters of water. How many liters of water did Pedro fill in the tank?
a. 30
b. 150
c. 300
d. 3,000
e. 30,000

24. A recipe calls for x fluid ounces of milk. Which algebraic expression represents how many cups of milk will be needed for this dish?
a. $\frac{1}{4}x$
b. $\frac{3}{4}x$
c. $\frac{1}{7}x$
d. $\frac{1}{8}x$
e. $\frac{7}{8}x$

25. Which expression has the same value as $y^4 \times y^5$?
a. y^9
b. y^{20}
c. $2y^9$
d. $2y^{20}$
e. $9y$

Answers and Explanations

Part I

1. a. The coefficient of this number is 1.4 because the coefficient must always be a number with an absolute value greater than one but less than ten. The base is always written as the exponent of 10. This number can be determined by counting the number of places after the decimal. Four groups of three zeros each is 12 (4 groups of 3, or 4×3), and then one more is added to get the decimal between the 1 and the 4. That makes 13 places total, so the answer is 1.4×10^{13}.

2. c. Towns A, B, C, and D form two right triangles. To determine the distance between Towns B and D, or the hypotenuse of the right triangle formed by Towns B, C, and D, apply the Pythagorean Theorem.

$a^2 + b^2 = c^2$

$6^2 + 8^2 = c^2$

$36 + 64 = c^2$

$100 = c^2$

$10 \text{ mi} = c$

Town B and Town D are 10 miles apart.

3. c. Supplementary angles are two angles whose combined measures are 18°. $\angle$e and $\angle$g are supplementary angles because they create a straight line, which has an angle measure of 180°.

4. a. Alternate interior angles are always equal in measure. Since $\angle$e and $\angle$d are alternate interior angles, formed by a backward Z, and $m\angle e = 64°$, then $m\angle d = 64°$.

5. b. Use the distance formula or count the number of units to determine the length and width of the rectangle. The rectangle is 4 units long and 3 units wide. The area of this rectangle is (length)(width) = (4 units)(3 units) = 12 units squared.

6. a. The x-axis forms the line of reflection because the x-coordinates of each point remain the same.

7. **Answer:** See coordinate grid below. Use $r_{y\text{-axis}}(x,y) = (-x,y)$ to determine the coordinates of the new figure. You may also count the number of units to the line of reflection to determine the coordinates of the new figure. The coordinates of the rectangle MNOP are $(-1,-2)$, $(-5,-2)$, $(-5,-5)$, and $(-1,-5)$.

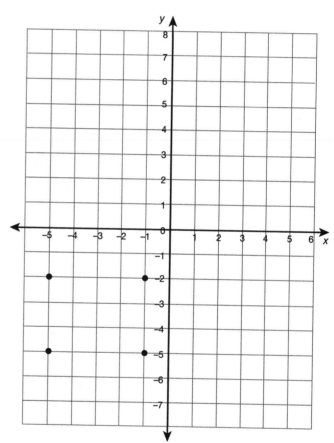

8. d. Use the distance formula, Distance = rate × time, to determine the rate.

$D = r \times t$

$D = 500$ miles and $t = 8$ hours

$500 = r \times 8$

$\frac{500}{8} = r$

62.5 miles per hour $= r$

David must drive approximately 60 miles per hour, when rounded to the nearest ten.

9. Answer:

Use the volume formula for a rectangular solid, $V = $ length × width × height, to determine the volume of the original figure: (2 feet)(4 feet)(8 feet) = 64 feet³. A container that is double that volume contains 128 feet³.

10. e. The number to the right of the hundreds place is 7. Because 7 is greater than 5, 4,378 must be rounded up to 4,400.

11. c. Write each group of digits from left to right, stopping at each comma to add a comma in the number. This is the only answer that expresses the thousands amount correctly, so if you noticed that, you could have used the process of elimination to pick the correct answer.

12. Answer:

To add $5\frac{1}{2}$ and $6\frac{1}{4}$, find the lowest common denominator (4) and change to like fractions. Add the fractions ($\frac{2}{4} + \frac{1}{4} = \frac{3}{4}$) and then add the whole numbers (5 + 6 = 11). The answer is $11\frac{3}{4}$. However, you cannot express mixed fractions using a standard grid, so this number must be converted to 11.75 or the improper fraction $\frac{47}{4}$.

13. a. To find the perimeter of the garden, use the formula Perimeter = 2(length × width). Since you can use a calculator, it might be easier to convert the fractions into decimals, so your formula is:

$P = 2(12.5 + 16.125)$

$P = 2(28.625)$

$P = 57.25$ feet

Mr. Osaka will need to purchase $57\frac{1}{4}$ feet of fencing.

14. e. The total amount of sales can be determined by multiplying the quantity of each item and its cost and adding the total of each item to determine the total amount of sales.

Total sales = 2($857.36) + 2 ($1,253.36)

Total sales = $1,714.72 + $2,506.72

Total sales = $4,221,44

15. e. The total amount of sales can be determined by multiplying the quantity of each item and its cost.

$1,253.36 × 4 = $5,013.44

16. c. The dessert preference ratio of cheesecake to ice cream is 15 to 40. In simplest terms, after dividing both numbers by 5, this ratio becomes 3:8.

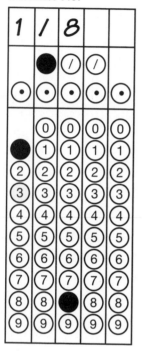

To convert 12.5% into a fraction, first convert the percentage into a decimal: 0.125. 0.125 can be written as $\frac{125}{1000}$, or $\frac{1}{8}$ in the simplest terms.

18. b. This problem tests your knowledge of the correct order of mathematical operations. Always use PEMDAS (parentheses, exponents, multiplication/division, addition/subtraction). First, multiply the two numbers in parentheses: $(2 × 12) = 24$. Second, do the multiplication operation of $20 × 2$ to get 40. Finally, do the rest of the addition and subtraction operations and get 141.

19.   Answer:

To determine the cost of 140 copies of John's presentation report, first figure out the cost of each report. Using the formula given:

$$\text{Total Cost} = c + \$0.125p + \$0.15$$
$$= \$0.15 + (\$0.125)(15) + \$0.15$$
$$= \$2.175$$

Each report costs $2.175. If there are 140 reports, then ($2.175)(140) = $304.50.

20. e. Factoring the algebraic expression results in $(x - 5)(x + 2) = 0$, meaning that {5, −2} are values of x that satisfy the equation. Alternatively, simply try out the answer choice values to see which ones satisfy the equation. If a number doesn't work (the equation isn't set to 0), you can eliminate any answer choice that has that value in it. When you substitute 5 and −2 for x in the equation, each number sets the equation equal to 0.

21. e. Locate −2 on a number line and move 8 units to the right. Mathematically:

$$-2° + 8° = 6°$$

22. a. If the team won 60% of its games, then it lost 40%, or 0.4, of the games.

$0.4 \times 80 = 32$ games lost

Choice **c** is how many games the team won last season.

23. c. Use the simple interest formula Interest = principal × rate × time, or in this case, Interest = $2,350 \times 0.0625 \times 3 = \$440.625$. Then add this number to the principal: $\$2,350 + \$440.625 = \$2,790.625$. Over three years, Jack will have to pay back $2,790.63 for his loan.

24. a. Variable *y*, or a number, divided by sixteen equals four.

25. Answer:

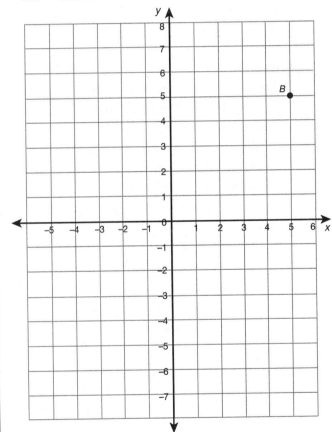

To create a rectangle, opposite sides must have equal length and be parallel to each other. On a coordinate grid, this means that point *B* has to have the *x*-value of point *D* and the *y*-value of point *A*.

Part II

1. Answer:

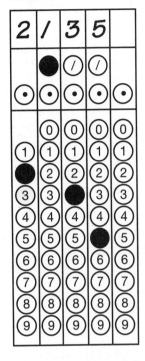

To find the slope of this equation, solve for *y*.

$2x - 3y - 9 = 0$

$-3y - 9 = -2$

$-3y = -2x + 9$

$y = \frac{2}{3}x - 3$

The slope of this equation is $\frac{2}{3}$.

2. c. To find out the how much weight that Adam needs to remove from his luggage, subtract the weight requirement (50 lb) from his current luggage weight (87 lb): 87 lb − 50 lb = *w*.

3. d. To find the median of a set of numbers, put the numbers in ascending order.

77, 117, 165, 198, 198

The middle number, 165, is the median.

4. d. To add $34\frac{1}{2}$ and $12\frac{1}{4}$, find the lowest common denominator (4) and change the fractions to like fractions. Add the fractions $(\frac{1}{4} + \frac{2}{4} = \frac{3}{4})$ and then add the whole numbers $(34 + 12 = 46)$. The sum is $46\frac{3}{4}$.

5. c. To subtract $1\frac{3}{4}$ from $34\frac{1}{4}$, first change $34\frac{1}{4}$ to $33\frac{5}{4}$. Next, subtract the fractions $(\frac{5}{4} - \frac{3}{4} = \frac{2}{4} = \frac{1}{2})$, then subtract the whole numbers $(33 - 1 = 32)$. The difference is $32\frac{1}{2}$.

6. b. Substitute the algebraic expressions into the formula for the area of a triangle, Area $= \frac{1}{2} \times$ base $\times$ height.

Area $= \frac{1}{2} \times 2x \times 5x$

Area $= \frac{10x^2}{2}$

Area $= 5x^2$

7. b. The distance formula is Distance = rate × time. We are given the distance Carmelo will travel (25 miles) and are asked to find the time it will take him to finish, so knowing the rate of travel is necessary to use the formula and find out the time it will take for Carmelo to finish this trail.

8. c. There are four white cards, one gray card, and two black cards. This makes 7 cards total, 3 of which are not white. Therefore, the probability of picking a nonwhite card is 3 out of 7, or $\frac{3}{7}$.

9. d. Use the following proportion to solve for n, which is the actual distance in miles.

$\frac{2}{40} = \frac{5}{n}$

$2n = (5)(40)$

$2n = 200$

$n = 100$ miles

So, the actual distance between Town A and Town B is 100 miles.

10. a. To find the amount of money Daquan has left after paying for lunches during football camp, subtract $5x$ (the cost of lunch for five days, which is five times the cost of lunch for one day) from $75. The equation is $m = \$75 - 5x$.

11. b. Lines are parallel to one another when they have the same slope. Since the slope of line $y = \frac{1}{2}x + 8$ is $\frac{1}{2}$, the parallel line must have a slope of $\frac{1}{2}$ also. The only other line with a slope of $\frac{1}{2}$ is $y = \frac{1}{2}x - 8$.

12. a. Cross multiply to solve for n.

$\frac{5}{6} = \frac{n}{12}$

$6n = (5)(12)$

$6n = 60$

$n = 10$

13. b. To find out the percentage of money devoted to taxation, divide $195 by $1,500: $195 ÷ $1,500 = 0.13. Convert 0.13 into a percentage by multiplying the decimal by 100, which gives 13%.

14. b. Find out the discount of the speaker system by multiplying $234 by 0.25 (the decimal equivalent of 25%): $234 × 0.25 = $58.50. Subtract that figure from the original price to get the discounted price: $234.00 − $58.50 = $175.50.

15. c. To find out how many miles Johnny traveled from weeks 3 through 5, look at the line graph and add the values for those three weeks: 36.2 miles + 52.25 miles + 12.25 miles = 100.7 miles.

16. d. To find out how many more miles Johnny traveled in week 4 than in week 5, subtract the distance he traveled in week 5 from the distance he traveled in week 4: 52.25 miles − 12.25 miles = 40 miles.

17. **Answer:**

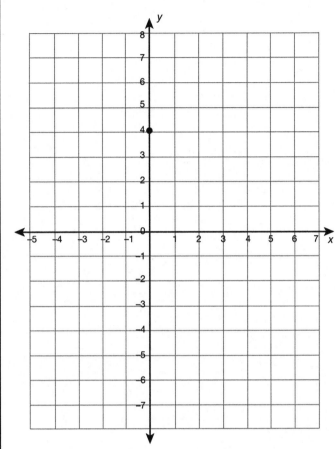

The y-intercept is the place where a line crosses the y-axis. At this point, the value of x must be 0 because the y-axis crosses the x-axis at $x = 0$. Therefore, plug the value $x = 0$ into the equation $y = 3x + 4$ to find the value of y: $y = 3(0) + 4$, so $y = 4$. The point where the line crosses the y-axis is (0,4).

18. a. Use the distance between points formula to determine the distance between point A $(-7,0)$ and point B $(1,6)$. You could also sketch out a grid if that helps you visualize the two points.

$$d = \sqrt{(x_2 - x_1)^2 + (y_2 - y_1)^2}$$
$$d = \sqrt{(1 - (-7))^2 + (6 - 0)^2}$$
$$d = \sqrt{(8)^2 + (6)^2}$$
$$d = \sqrt{64 + 36}$$
$$d = \sqrt{100}$$
$$d = 10$$

Points A and B are 10 units apart.

19. a. To determine the total cost of these items, add the costs of 2 bags of lollipops ($2 \times \$2.25$) and 4 boxes of chocolate ($4 \times \$5.45$).

20. d. The mode is the value that occurs most often within a set of numbers. The number 2,300 occurs twice, so it is the mode.

21. Answer:

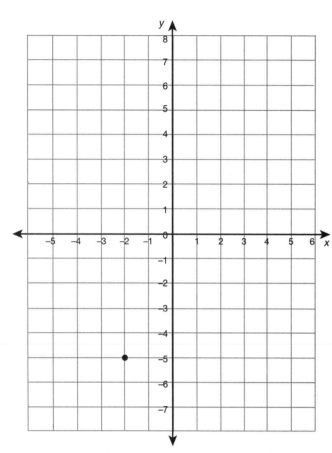

Remember that with any coordinate, the *x*-value comes first. Since this value is negative, you must first move two units to the left of the origin. Next, since the *y*-value is also negative, you move five units down from there. This is the point (−2,−5).

22. a. Using the distributive property $a(b + c)$ $= ab + ac$, multiply $8m$ by $2m$ and by -1 to yield $16m^2 - 8m$.

23. d. There are 1,000 milliliters in one liter. Convert milliliters into liters by dividing the number of milliliters by 1,000: 3,000,000 milliliters ÷ 1,000 milliliters per liter = 3,000 liters.

24. d. There are 8 fluid ounces in a cup. The algebraic expression to determine the number of cups in *x* fluid ounces is $\frac{1}{8}x$.

25. a. To multiply $y^4 \times y^5$, add their exponents: $4 + 5 = 9$. Therefore, the product is y^9.

Question Breakdown

Question	Standard
Part I	
1.	Number Sense and Operations
2.	Measurement and Geometry
3.	Measurement and Geometry
4.	Measurement and Geometry
5.	Measurement and Geometry
6.	Measurement and Geometry
7.	Measurement and Geometry
8.	Measurement and Geometry
9.	Measurement and Geometry
10.	Number Sense and Operations
11.	Number Sense and Operations
12.	Number Sense and Operations
13.	Number Sense and Operations
14.	Data Analysis
15.	Data Analysis
16.	Data Analysis
17.	Number Sense and Operations
18.	Number Sense and Operations
19.	Number Sense and Operations
20.	Algebra
21.	Number Sense and Operations
22.	Number Sense and Operations
23.	Number Sense and Operations
24.	Algebra
25.	Measurement and Geometry
Part II	
1.	Algebra
2.	Algebra
3.	Data Analysis
4.	Data Analysis
5.	Data Analysis
6.	Algebra
7.	Measurement and Geometry
8.	Data Analysis
9.	Measurement and Geometry
10.	Algebra
11.	Measurement and Geometry
12.	Algebra
13.	Number Sense and Operations
14.	Number Sense and Operations
15.	Data Analysis
16.	Data Analysis
17.	Measurement and Geometry
18.	Measurement and Geometry
19.	Number Sense and Operations
20.	Number Sense and Operations
21.	Measurement and Geometry
22.	Algebra
23.	Number Sense and Operations
24.	Algebra
25.	Algebra

CHAPTER

9 ▶ PRACTICE TEST 2

This is the second of two practice tests based on the GED® Math Test. After working through the review in Chapters 3–7, take this test to see how much your score has improved from the Diagnostic Test.

You are now familiar with the kinds of questions and answer formats you will see on the official GED® Test. Now take this posttest to identify any areas that you may need to review in more depth before the test day. When you are finished, check the answers on page 172 carefully to assess your results. Remember to:

- Work carefully
- Use estimation to eliminate answer choices or to check your work
- Answer every question
- Check to make sure your answers are logical
- Use the formula cheat sheet on pages 179 and 180, when needed

To simulate the test conditions, use the time constraints of the official GED® Mathematics Test. Allow 45 minutes for Part I. You may use a calculator to answer these 25 questions. Then, give yourself 45 minutes for Part II. You should not use a calculator for these 25 questions.

Remember, on the official GED® Test, an unanswered question is counted as incorrect, so make a good guess on questions you're not sure about.

Directions: Read each of the following questions carefully and determine the best answer. Record your answers by filling in the circles on the answer sheet provided for multiple-choice and alternative-format questions.

Note: On the GED® Test, you are not permitted to write in the test booklet. For this pretest, practice by making any notes or calculations on a separate piece of paper.

Part I

1.	ⓐ	ⓑ	ⓒ	ⓓ	ⓔ	10.	ⓐ	ⓑ	ⓒ	ⓓ	ⓔ	19.	ⓐ	ⓑ	ⓒ ⓓ ⓔ
2.	ⓐ	ⓑ	ⓒ	ⓓ	ⓔ	11.	ⓐ	ⓑ	ⓒ	ⓓ	ⓔ	20.	ⓐ	ⓑ	ⓒ ⓓ ⓔ
3.	ⓐ	ⓑ	ⓒ	ⓓ	ⓔ	12.	ⓐ	ⓑ	ⓒ	ⓓ	ⓔ	21.	ⓐ	ⓑ	ⓒ ⓓ ⓔ
4.	ⓐ	ⓑ	ⓒ	ⓓ	ⓔ	13.	ⓐ	ⓑ	ⓒ	ⓓ	ⓔ	22.	ⓐ	ⓑ	ⓒ ⓓ ⓔ
5.	ⓐ	ⓑ	ⓒ	ⓓ	ⓔ	14.	ⓐ	ⓑ	ⓒ	ⓓ	ⓔ	23.	ⓐ	ⓑ	ⓒ ⓓ ⓔ
6.	ⓐ	ⓑ	ⓒ	ⓓ	ⓔ	15.	ⓐ	ⓑ	ⓒ	ⓓ	ⓔ	24.	ⓐ	ⓑ	ⓒ ⓓ ⓔ
7.	ⓐ	ⓑ	ⓒ	ⓓ	ⓔ	16.	ⓐ	ⓑ	ⓒ	ⓓ	ⓔ	25.	ⓐ	ⓑ	ⓒ ⓓ ⓔ
8.	ⓐ	ⓑ	ⓒ	ⓓ	ⓔ	17.	ⓐ	ⓑ	ⓒ	ⓓ	ⓔ				
9.	ⓐ	ⓑ	ⓒ	ⓓ	ⓔ	18.	ⓐ	ⓑ	ⓒ	ⓓ	ⓔ				

Part II

1.	ⓐ	ⓑ	ⓒ	ⓓ	ⓔ	10.	ⓐ	ⓑ	ⓒ	ⓓ	ⓔ	19.	ⓐ	ⓑ	ⓒ ⓓ ⓔ
2.	ⓐ	ⓑ	ⓒ	ⓓ	ⓔ	11.	ⓐ	ⓑ	ⓒ	ⓓ	ⓔ	20.	ⓐ	ⓑ	ⓒ ⓓ ⓔ
3.	ⓐ	ⓑ	ⓒ	ⓓ	ⓔ	12.	ⓐ	ⓑ	ⓒ	ⓓ	ⓔ	21.	ⓐ	ⓑ	ⓒ ⓓ ⓔ
4.	ⓐ	ⓑ	ⓒ	ⓓ	ⓔ	13.	ⓐ	ⓑ	ⓒ	ⓓ	ⓔ	22.	ⓐ	ⓑ	ⓒ ⓓ ⓔ
5.	ⓐ	ⓑ	ⓒ	ⓓ	ⓔ	14.	ⓐ	ⓑ	ⓒ	ⓓ	ⓔ	23.	ⓐ	ⓑ	ⓒ ⓓ ⓔ
6.	ⓐ	ⓑ	ⓒ	ⓓ	ⓔ	15.	ⓐ	ⓑ	ⓒ	ⓓ	ⓔ	24.	ⓐ	ⓑ	ⓒ ⓓ ⓔ
7.	ⓐ	ⓑ	ⓒ	ⓓ	ⓔ	16.	ⓐ	ⓑ	ⓒ	ⓓ	ⓔ	25.	ⓐ	ⓑ	ⓒ ⓓ ⓔ
8.	ⓐ	ⓑ	ⓒ	ⓓ	ⓔ	17.	ⓐ	ⓑ	ⓒ	ⓓ	ⓔ				
9.	ⓐ	ⓑ	ⓒ	ⓓ	ⓔ	18.	ⓐ	ⓑ	ⓒ	ⓓ	ⓔ				

Part I—Calculator Allowed

You have 45 minutes to complete the following 25 questions.

1. What is 72.037 written in word form?
   a. seventy-two and thirty-seven
   b. seventy-two thousand thirty-seven
   c. seventy-two and thirty-seven hundredths
   d. seventy-two and thirty-seven thousandths
   e. seventy-two thousand thirty-seven hundredths

2. The coordinates of Point W are $(-5,-3)$. What is the location of Point W?

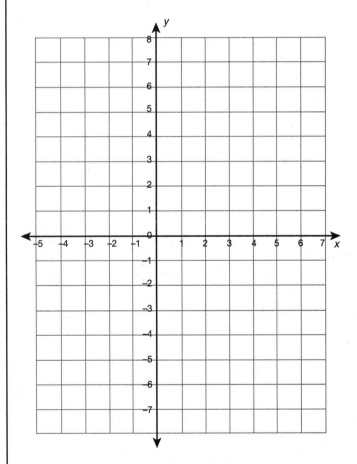

3. $\angle 1$ and $\angle 2$ are complementary angles. If $m\angle 1 = 25°$, what is $m\angle 2$?
   a. 25°
   b. 55°
   c. 65°
   d. 145°
   e. 155°

4. Which value correctly completes the table?

x	$\frac{1}{4}x + 4x$
2	$8\frac{1}{2}$
3	$12\frac{3}{4}$
4	?

   a. 1
   b. 12
   c. 16
   d. 17
   e. 18

5. What is the area of the parallelogram?

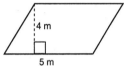

   a. 25 m²
   b. 20 m²
   c. 18 m²
   d. 16 m²
   e. 10 m²

6. David is completing y number of hours of his internship requirements. Which algebraic expression represents how many minutes of internship requirements he will need to complete?

   a. $\frac{1}{60}y$

   b. $60y$

   c. $24y$

   d. $12y$

   e. $\frac{1}{24}y$

7. Evaluate: $\sqrt{81}$

   a. 8

   b. 9

   c. Between 7 and 8

   d. Between 8 and 9

   e. Between 9 and 10

Questions 8 through 10 refer to the following bar graph that shows the average life span of different animals.

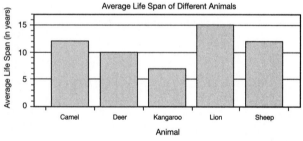

Source: www.pubquizhelp.com

8. Which animal has the shortest average life span?

   a. Camel

   b. Deer

   c. Kangaroo

   d. Lion

   e. Sheep

9. About how much longer is the average life span of a camel than that of a deer?

   a. 2 years

   b. 3 years

   c. 4 years

   d. 5 years

   e. 6 years

10. Which two animals have the same average life span?

   a. Camel and Lion

   b. Deer and Camel

   c. Kangaroo and Sheep

   d. Lion and Deer

   e. Sheep and Camel

11. Evaluate: $8 + (1 + 5)^2 \div 4$

   a. 7

   b. 11

   c. 17

   d. 8.5

   e. 15.25

12. There are 75 staff members at Johnson Elementary School. 50 of these staff members are teachers. What fraction of the staff are teachers?

   a. $\frac{1}{5}$

   b. $\frac{1}{4}$

   c. $\frac{1}{3}$

   d. $\frac{2}{3}$

   e. $\frac{3}{4}$

13. Simplify: $3(2g + 4h)$

   a. $9gh$

   b. $18gh$

   c. $5g + 7h$

   d. $6g + 4h$

   e. $6g + 12h$

14. Jackson Elementary School is building a fence around the playground shown below. What is the total amount of fencing needed to complete this project?

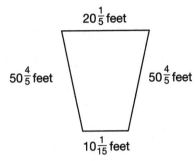

$20\frac{1}{5}$ feet

$50\frac{4}{5}$ feet $50\frac{4}{5}$ feet

$10\frac{1}{15}$ feet

   a. $131\frac{13}{15}$ feet

   b. $131\frac{3}{15}$ feet

   c. $131\frac{3}{5}$ feet

   d. $131\frac{10}{15}$ feet

   e. $131\frac{3}{10}$ feet

15. Solve for x.

$\frac{4}{5} = \frac{x}{20}$

   a. 16
   b. 19
   c. 25
   d. 30
   e. 36

16. Nelson drove $50\frac{1}{5}$ miles yesterday and $125\frac{1}{8}$ miles today. How many miles did Nelson drive?

Mark your answer on the answer grid, rounding to the nearest tenth.

17. The boy-to-girl ratio of Vicksburg Elementary School is 5 to 3. The total population is 800. How many boys are there in Vicksburg Elementary School?

   a. 300
   b. 400
   c. 500
   d. 600
   e. 800

18. Order $\frac{3}{4}, \frac{3}{8}, \frac{1}{2}$, and $\frac{1}{4}$ from greatest to least.

   a. $\frac{1}{2}, \frac{3}{4}, \frac{1}{4}, \frac{3}{8}$

   b. $\frac{1}{2}, \frac{3}{8}, \frac{3}{4}, \frac{1}{4}$

   c. $\frac{1}{4}, \frac{3}{4}, \frac{1}{2}, \frac{3}{8}$

   d. $\frac{3}{4}, \frac{1}{2}, \frac{3}{8}, \frac{1}{4}$

   e. $\frac{3}{8}, \frac{3}{4}, \frac{1}{4}, \frac{1}{2}$

19. Write $\frac{7}{20}$ as a decimal. Mark your answer on the answer grid.

20. Suppose Mason needs to cut a piece of wood board measuring $18\frac{2}{5}$ feet into 4 equal pieces. What is the length of each wood board?

Mark your answer on the answer grid.

21. What is the value of y for the equation $y = x^2 - 3x + 12$ if $x = 4$?

a. 16
b. 17
c. 20
d. 25
e. 30

Questions 22 through 24 refer to the following table that shows the nutrition facts for five types of vegetables.

Nutrition Facts			
Vegetable (serving size)	Calories	Sodium (mg)	Potassium (mg)
Bell Pepper (1 medium)	25	40	220
Broccoli (1 medium stalk)	45	80	460
Onion (1 medium)	45	5	190
Potato (1 medium)	110	0	620
Tomato (1 medium)	25	20	340

Source: U.S. Census Bureau.

22. How many calories are in one medium-sized potato?

  a. 0

  b. 20

  c. 45

  d. 110

  e. 620

23. How many more milligrams of potassium does one medium stalk of broccoli have than one medium bell pepper?

  a. 220

  b. 240

  c. 400

  d. 460

  e. 680

24. Which vegetable has the lowest amount of sodium?

  a. Bell pepper

  b. Broccoli

  c. Onion

  d. Potato

  e. Tomato

25. What is the length of the hypotenuse of the right triangle?

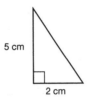

  a. $\sqrt{29}$ cm

  b. $\sqrt{15}$ cm

  c. $\sqrt{10}$ cm

  d. $\sqrt{7}$ cm

  e. $\sqrt{3}$ cm

STOP. DO NOT PROCEED TO THE NEXT SECTION UNTIL THE 45 MINUTES FOR PART I ARE COMPLETED.

Part II—NO Calculator

You have 45 minutes to complete the following 25 questions.

1. What is the approximate volume of the cylinder in square centimeters?

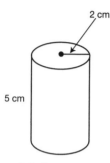

2 cm

5 cm

Mark your answer in the answer grid.

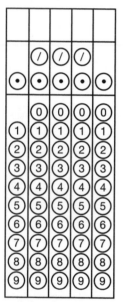

2. Gerry bought gifts for four of his friends. Two of his friends will each receive a book at x dollars. The other two friends will receive a vase at y dollars. Which algebraic expression best represents the amount of money Gerry spent on gifts?
   a. $2x + 2y$
   b. $4x + 4y$
   c. $2x \times 2y$
   d. $4x \times 4y$
   e. $12x + 12y$

3. What is 16% of 20?
   a. 0.008
   b. 0.8
   c. 0.32
   d. 1.25
   e. 3.2

4. Which two values satisfy the equation $x^2 + 6x - 7 = 0$?
   a. $\{6,1\}$
   b. $\{-7,1\}$
   c. $\{7,1\}$
   d. $\{5,2\}$
   e. $\{5,-2\}$

Question 5 refers to the following coordinate plane.

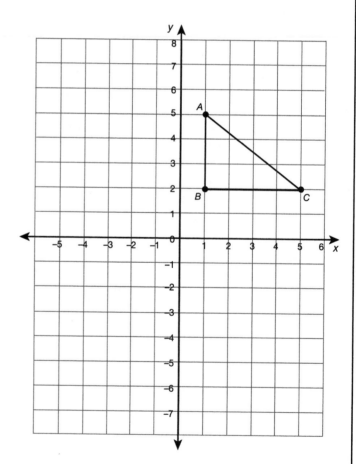

5. Show the location of triangle *XYZ*, a reflection of triangle *ABC* over the *y*-axis.

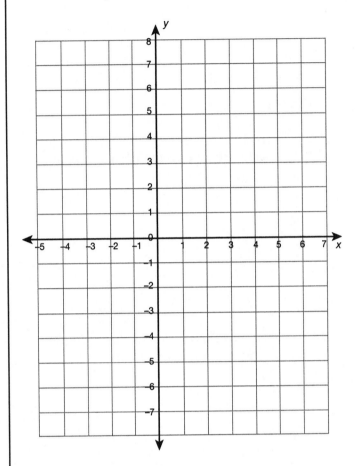

Questions 6 and 7 refer to the following illustration.

Rodrigo rolls a six-sided number cube.

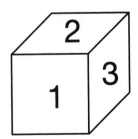

6. What is the probability that he will roll an even number?

   a. $\frac{1}{2}$

   b. $\frac{1}{3}$

   c. $\frac{1}{4}$

   d. $\frac{1}{5}$

   e. $\frac{1}{6}$

7. If Rodrigo rolls the number cube 100 times, how many times should he expect to roll an even number?

8. Which fraction is equivalent to the decimal 1.8?

   a. $1\frac{4}{5}$

   b. $1\frac{2}{5}$

   c. $1\frac{8}{5}$

   d. $1\frac{4}{10}$

   e. $1\frac{8}{15}$

Question 9 refers to the following illustration.

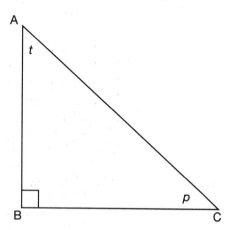

9. What is the sum of angles t and p?

a. 45°

b. 90°

c. 180°

d. 270°

e. 360°

10. A bicycle trail in Byers Park is $50\frac{1}{4}$ miles long. If Joanne can bike 5 miles per hour, how many hours will she need to complete the trail?

a. 10

b. $10\frac{1}{10}$

c. $10\frac{1}{20}$

d. $10\frac{1}{2}$

e. $10\frac{1}{40}$

11. Which is a solution to $5y - 5 \leq 6$?

a. 2

b. 3

c. 4

d. 5

e. 6

12. Write $4\frac{2}{5}$ as an improper fraction.

a. $\frac{6}{5}$

b. $\frac{8}{5}$

c. $\frac{11}{5}$

d. $\frac{18}{5}$

e. $\frac{22}{5}$

13. Which algebraic expression can be used to represent the quotient of thirteen and three times a number?

a. $\frac{13}{3x}$

b. $\frac{1}{3x} - 13$

c. $\frac{13}{x} - 13$

d. $\frac{1}{3} - x$

e. $\frac{1}{13} - x$

14. Which is the missing value for this equation?

$18\ g = \boxed{?}\ kg$

a. 0.18

b. 0.018

c. 180

d. 1,800

e. 18,000

15. Show the location of the figure that is formed by points (1,8), (1,2) and (7,2) on the coordinate plane grid.

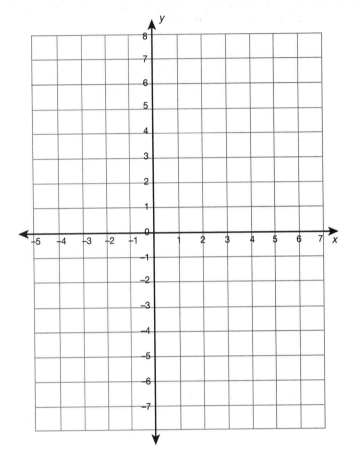

16. Mr. Carson taught five classes at Aviation High School today. He recorded the attendance of these classes in the following chart.

Periods	Attendance
Period 1	25
Period 3	30
Period 4	25
Period 5	35
Period 7	y

If the average (mean) attendance today for Mr. Carson's classes is 31, how many students are in his Period 7 class?

a. 25
b. 31
c. 40
d. 41
e. 50

17. Each 1.75-pound cake mix package can bake one cake. Which expression can be used to find how many pounds of cake mix are needed to bake 15 cakes?

a. $15 \div 1.75$
b. $15 + 1.75$
c. 15×1.75
d. $(15 \div 1.75) \times 15$
e. $15 \times 1.75 \times 15$

Questions 18 and 19 refer to the following graph.

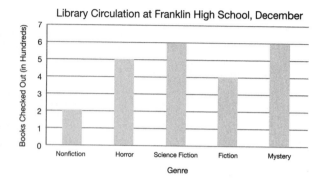

18. What is the total number of books in circulation at Franklin High School in December?
    a. 23
    b. 230
    c. 1,200
    d. 2,300
    e. 4,600

19. Rounded to the nearest percent, what percentage of the books checked out in December were nonfiction? Mark your answer in the answer grid.

Question 20 refers to the illustration on the following coordinate plane.

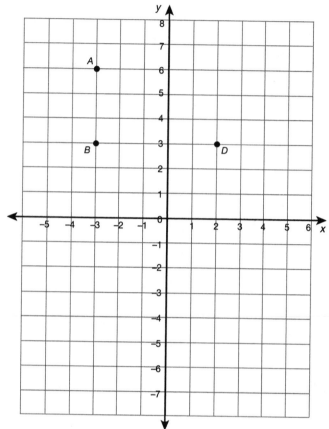

20. Mark on the coordinate plane grid to illustrate point *C* that completes the rectangle *ABCD*.

21. Mary saved $24 dollars on a computer monitor at an appliance store. The discount is 25%. What is the original price?
    a. $6
    b. $96
    c. $600
    d. $120
    e. $150

22. The names of the following students will be drawn at random to win a prize. What is the probability of a person whose name starts with J winning the prize?

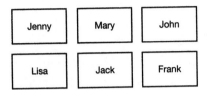

| Jenny | Mary | John |
| Lisa | Jack | Frank |

a. 10%
b. 20%
c. 40%
d. 50%
e. 100%

Question 23 refers to the following graphs.

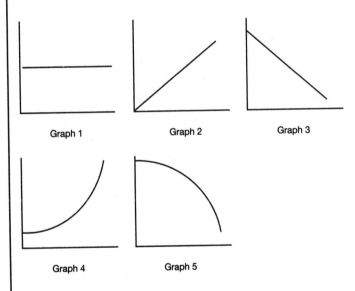

Graph 1   Graph 2   Graph 3

Graph 4   Graph 5

23. The price of a certain product has not changed over a five-year period. Which graph can best be used to represent this data? (Assume Price is the vertical axis and Time is the horizontal axis.)
a. Graph 1
b. Graph 2
c. Graph 3
d. Graph 4
e. Graph 5

24. Of 2,800 students surveyed, 28% prefer butter pecan ice cream over other flavors. How many students prefer butter pecan ice cream?
a. 100
b. 280
c. 784
d. 1,567
e. 2,358

25. Show the location of the coordinates on the coordinate grid for the equation $y = 4x - 10$, when $x = 2$.

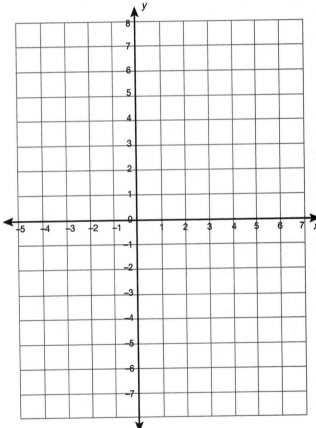

Answers and Explanations

Part I

1. d. To represent a decimal in words, first state the whole number and then state the final place value name. The whole number is "seventy two," and then you say "and" to represent the decimal before continuing right. Knowing this, you can eliminate choices **b** and **e** because those choices do not include "and." The number farthest to the right after the decimal (7) is in the thousandths place, so the decimal is "thirty-seven thousandths," eliminating choices **a** and **c**.

2. Answer:

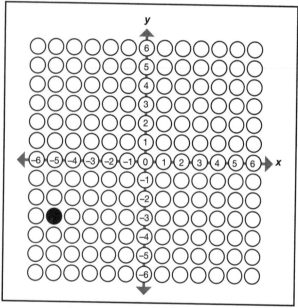

Since both the *x* and *y* values are negative, you must first head left (not right) five units along the *x*-axis, and then down (not up) three units from that point.

3. c. Complementary angles are two angles whose measures add to 90 degrees. If $\angle 1$ and $\angle 2$ are complimentary angles, then $90° - 25° = m\angle 2 = 65°$.

4. d. To find out the missing value in the table, substitute 4 for *x* in the initial equation.

$$? = \tfrac{1}{4}x + 4x$$
$$? = \tfrac{1}{4}(4) + 4(4)$$
$$? = 1 + 16$$
$$? = 17$$

5. b. Use the area formula for a parallelogram to determine its area. Remember that this can be found in the Formulas Chart. For a parallelogram, Area = (base)(height); in this case, Area = (base)(height) = (5 m)(4 m) = 20 m².

6. b. There are 60 minutes in one hour. To find out how many minutes are in a certain number of hours, multiply the number of hours by 60. The number of minutes in *y* hours is 60*y*.

7. b. 81 is a perfect square of 9 × 9. The square root of 81 is 9.

8. c. The animal with the shortest life span is the animal with the shortest bar on the graph. This is the kangaroo.

9. a. This is a common two-step data analysis problem. For Step 1, you must read the graph correctly and determine the average life span of both the camel and the deer. Looking at the graph, the average life span of a camel is 12 years, while that of a deer is 10 years. For step 2, you must perform some mathematic operation, in this case subtracting the average life span of a deer from that of a camel. Since 12 years − 10 years = 2 years, the answer is **a**.

10. e. The two animals with the same average life span are the sheep and the camel. You can tell this because their bars are the same height, and on a bar graph, two bars that are the same height have the same value.

11. c. This problem tests your knowledge of the correct order of mathematical operations. Always use PEMDAS (parentheses, exponents, multiplication/division, addition/subtraction). First, add the numbers in parentheses: $(1 + 5) = 6$. Then, evaluate all exponents, in this case by squaring 6: $6^2 = 6 \times 6 = 36$. Then, divide 36 by 4 and get 9. Finally, do the addition operation and get $8 + 9 = 17$.

12. d. 50 out of 75, or $\frac{50}{73}$, staff members are teachers. The largest common factor of 50 and 75 is 25. Divide both 50 and 75 by 25 to reduce the fraction to $\frac{2}{3}$.

13. e. Since g and h are two different variables separated in the parentheses by an addition sign, there is no way to combine them more than they are already. This eliminates choices **a** and **b**, which could only be reached by multiplying the variables, never by adding them. Using the distributive property $a(b + c) = ab + bc$, multiply 3 by $2g$ and $4h$ and retain the addition sign.

14. a. To determine the perimeter of the playground, add the length of each side. The difficult part here is that some of the fractions are different, but since you can use a calculator, you could always convert all of the fractions to decimals and then add the numbers together. Or, find the lowest common denominator (LCD) of the fractions, which is 15, and add them.

$20\frac{3}{15} + 50\frac{12}{15} + 50\frac{12}{15} + 10\frac{1}{15} = 130\frac{28}{15} = 131\frac{13}{15}$ feet.

15. a. To solve for x, cross multiply:

$$\frac{4}{5} = \frac{x}{20}$$
$$(5)(x) = (4)(20)$$
$$5x = 80$$
$$\frac{5x}{5} = \frac{80}{5}$$
$$x = 16$$

16. Answer:

To add $50\frac{1}{5}$ and $125\frac{1}{8}$, first convert the fractions into decimals, and then add.
$50\frac{1}{5} + 125\frac{1}{8} = 50.2 + 125.125 = 175.325$ miles
Then round down to the nearest tenth.
$175.325 \approx 175.3$ miles

17. c. Use the following algebraic equations to determine the number of boys in the school.
$5x$ = the number of boys
$3x$ = the number of girls
$5x + 3x = 800$
$8x = 800$
$x = 100$
The number of boys in the school is
$5x = 5(100) = 500$.

18. d. To order the fractions from greatest to least, convert each fraction to a like fraction with the lowest common denominator, which is 8.

$$\frac{3}{4}, \frac{3}{8}, \frac{1}{2}, \frac{1}{4} \rightarrow \frac{6}{8}, \frac{3}{8}, \frac{4}{8}, \frac{2}{8}$$

Then you can easily sort them from greatest to least by their numerators: $\frac{6}{8}, \frac{3}{8}, \frac{4}{8}, \frac{2}{8}$, which is $\frac{3}{4}, \frac{1}{2}, \frac{3}{8}, \frac{1}{4}$ in the form presented in the question.

19. Answer:

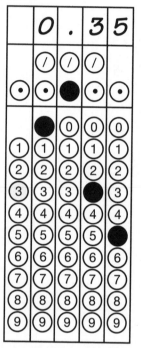

Use your calculator to divide 7 by 20. The answer is 0.35. Make sure you pencil in the decimal in the correct place on the answer grid.

20. Answer:

To divide $18\frac{2}{5}$ by 4, change the mixed number to an improper fraction, then divide by multiplying by the reciprocal of 4.

$$\frac{92}{5} \div \frac{4}{1} = \frac{92}{5} \times \frac{1}{4} = \frac{23}{5} \times \frac{1}{1} = \frac{23}{5}$$

Remember that you can place improper fractions into a standard grid, so $\frac{23}{5}$ is an acceptable answer.

21. a. Substitute $x = 4$ into the equation $y = x^2 - 3x + 12$.

$y = x^2 - 3x + 12$

$y = (4)(4) - (3)(4) + 12$

$y = 16 - 12 + 12$

$y = 16$

22. d. Locate the calories in one medium-sized potato on the table. This is the first column, not the second or third, both of which are incorrect choices waiting to catch you.

23. b. Locate the potassium column, which is on the far right, and find the values for one medium stalk of broccoli (460) and one medium bell pepper (220). Subtract the bell pepper value from the broccoli value: 460 mg − 220 mg = 240 mg.

24. d. Sodium is the middle column, and since the potato contains no sodium, it is the correct answer.

25. a. To determine the length of the hypotenuse of the right triangle, apply the Pythagorean Theorem.

$$a^2 + b^2 = c^2$$
$$5^2 + 2^2 = c^2$$
$$(5)(5) + (2)(2) = c^2$$
$$25 + 4 = c^2$$
$$29 = c^2$$
$$\sqrt{29} = c$$

Part II

1. **Answer:**

The volume of a cylinder is $\pi r^2 \times$ height. Remember that this can be found on the Formulas Chart, which also states that pi can be approximated to 3.14.

$V = \pi r^2 \times$ height
$V = (3.14)(2)(2) \times 6$
$V = 12.56 \times 6$
$V = 75.36$ cm^2

2. a. The algebraic expression for two books at x dollars is $2x$, while two vases at y dollars is $2y$. These two values are then added together, and the sum can be represented as $2x + 2y$.

3. e. Convert 16% into a decimal, which is 0.16. Multiply 0.16 by 20 and get 3.2.

4. b. While there is an algebraic method to determine the correct answer, you can also just try the values that appear in the answer choices. If one works (makes the equation equal 0), you can eliminate any answer choice that does not contain that number. If it doesn't work (does not make the equation equal 0), you can eliminate any answer choice that does contain that number. For instance, start with 1, since it appears in three different choices. Substituting 1 into the equation works, so choices **d** and **e** can be eliminated. Continuing with this method, substituting −7 into the equation also works, meaning that choice **b** must be correct.

5. Answer:

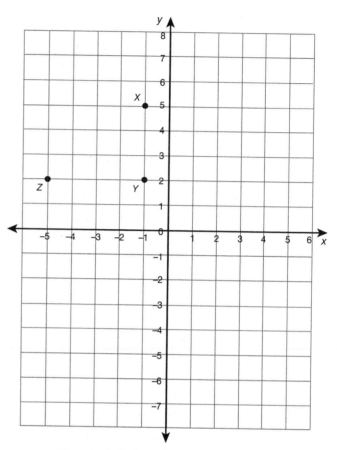

The *y*-axis is the vertical axis, so the reflected triangle will appear to the left of the existing triangle. While the *y*-axis values for all reflected points will be the same, the *x*-axis values will have the opposite sign, so *A* (1,5) will become reflected point *X* (−1,5); *B* (1,2) will become reflected point *Y* (−1,2); and *C* (5,2) will become reflected point *Z* (−5,2).

6. a. Half the numbers are even (2, 4, and 6). The odds of rolling an even number are 3 out of 6, or $\frac{1}{2}$.

7. Answer:

Half the numbers are even (2, 4, and 6). The odds of rolling an even number are 3 out of 6, or $\frac{1}{2}$. If Rodrigo rolled the number cube 100 times, he should expect to roll an even number 1 out of 2, or 50, times.

8. a. When converted to a fraction, 0.8 has a numerator of 8 and a denominator of 10. 1.8 can be converted into $1\frac{8}{10}$ or $1\frac{4}{5}$ in lowest terms.

9. b. The sum of all interior angles in a triangle is 180°. A right angle measures 90°. Therefore, the sum of the other two angles must be 90° because 90° + 90° = 180°.

10. c. Divide $50\frac{1}{4}$ by 5. Dividing 50 by 5 is the simpler part; it's dividing $\frac{1}{4}$ by 5 that can be tricky. Remember that 5 can be written as $\frac{5}{1}$, and that when dividing fractions, the divisor is flipped over and then multiplied.

$\frac{1}{4} \div 5$

$\frac{1}{4} \div \frac{5}{1}$

$\frac{1}{4} \times \frac{1}{5}$

$\frac{1}{20}$

$10\frac{1}{20}$

11. a. To search for an answer, you can substitute the values in the answer choices for y in the inequality. If you go this route, start with choice **c**, since this is the middle value. If that answer is too high, you know you need a lower number and can eliminate all higher numbers.

Alternatively, you can directly solve for y.

$5y - 5 \le 6$

$5y - 5 + 5 \le 6 + 5$

$5y \le 11$

$\frac{5y}{5} \le \frac{11}{5}$

$y \le 2\frac{1}{5}$

The only answer choice that satisfies this inequality is **a**.

12. e. To change a mixed number to an improper fraction, multiply the denominator by the whole number and then add the numerator. This number ($5 \times 4 + 2 = 22$) becomes the numerator of the improper fraction. The denominator (5) remains the same.

13. a. A quotient is the end result of division. 13 is the numerator and $3x$, or "three times a number," is the denominator.

14. b. There are 1,000 grams in a kilogram. Divide 18 by 1,000 and get 0.018. Of course, you do not actually have to divide. Instead, you can simply move the decimal point three places to the left.

15. Answer:

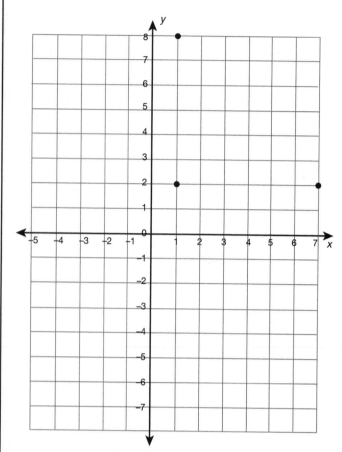

The figure is a right triangle.

16. c. To find the average (mean) attendance, add the students in all classes and then divide by the number of classes. Since the number of students in period 7 is unknown, use the variable y.

$$\frac{25 + 30 + 25 + 35 + y}{5} = 31$$

$$\frac{115 + y}{5} = 31$$

$$(5)\frac{115 + y}{5} = 31(5)$$

$$115 + y = 155$$

$$115 - 115 + y = 155 - 115$$

$$y = 40$$

So there are 40 students in Mr. Carson's Period 7 class.

17. c. To find the number of pounds of cake mix needed, multiply 15 (the number of cakes) by 1.75 (the number of pounds of cake mix needed to bake one cake).

18. d. Add the number of books checked out in each genre to find out the total number of books in circulation in December. In other words, add the heights of all the bars together. Also, realize that the number of "Books Checked Out" shown is "in Hundreds," so 23 is actually $23 \times 100 = 2{,}300$ books.

19. Answer:

9				
	/	/	/	
·	·	·	·	·
	0	0	0	0
1	1	1	1	1
2	2	2	2	2
3	3	3	3	3
4	4	4	4	4
5	5	5	5	5
6	6	6	6	6
7	7	7	7	7
8	8	8	8	8
●	9	9	9	9

200 out of 2,300 books checked out were nonfiction. This can be represented by $\frac{200}{2,300}$ or $\frac{2}{23}$ after simplification. Converting the fraction into a decimal gives 0.8595, which is 8.695%, or 9% when rounded to the nearest percentage.

20. Answer:

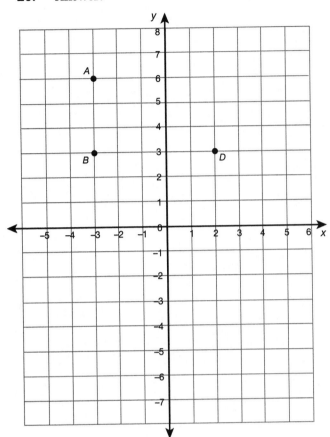

23. a. This problem looks difficult, but once you understand what it is asking, the idea is fairly simple. Graph 1 shows that the increase of time has no impact on the price. This is indicated by the straight horizontal line. In the other graphs, the line moves up or down, meaning that price (the vertical axis) moved up and down over time, which is not what the question asked for.

24. c. Convert 28% into a decimal and get 0.28. Multiply 0.28 by 2,800 students to get 784 students who prefer butter pecan ice cream.

25. Answer:

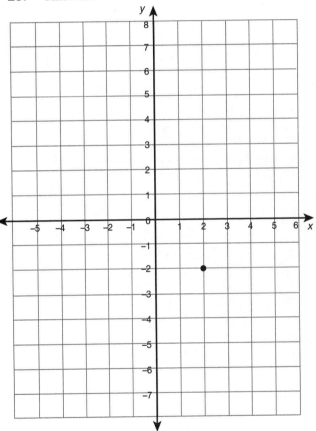

21. b. Use the following equation to solve this problem.

Original Price × Discount Rate = Discount

$$y \times 0.25 = \$24$$

$$\frac{0.25\,y}{0.25} = \frac{\$24}{0.25}$$

$$y = \$96$$

The original price of the computer monitor was $96. Be sure to remember that 25% equals 0.25, and the decimal must be used when doing calculations with percents.

22. d. There are six cards, and three people have names that begin with a J. This means the probability is $\frac{3}{6}$, or $\frac{1}{2} \cdot \frac{1}{2} = 0.50 = 50\%$.

Although this problem seems difficult, you can easily answer it by following directions. Plug the value $x = 2$ into the equation, and then find out the corresponding value for y.

$$y = 4x - 10$$
$$y = 4(2) - 10$$
$$y = 8 - 10$$
$$y = -2$$

Now mark point $(2, -2)$ on the coordinate grid.

Question Breakdown

Question	Standard
Part I	
1	Number Sense and Operations
2	Geometry and Measurement
3	Geometry and Measurement
4	Algebra
5	Geometry and Measurement
6	Algebra
7	Number Sense and Operations
8	Data Analysis
9	Data Analysis
10	Data Analysis
11	Number Sense and Operations
12	Number Sense and Operations
13	Algebra
14	Geometry and Measurement
15	Algebra
16	Number Sense and Operations
17	Number Sense and Operations
18	Number Sense and Operations
19	Number Sense and Operations
20	Number Sense and Operations
21	Algebra
22	Data Analysis
23	Data Analysis
24	Data Analysis
25	Geometry and Measurement

Part II	
1	Geometry and Measurement
2	Algebra
3	Number Sense and Operations
4	Algebra
5	Geometry and Measurement
6	Data Analysis
7	Number Sense and Operations
8	Number Sense and Operations
9	Geometry and Measurement
10	Number Sense and Operations
11	Algebra
12	Number Sense and Operations
13	Algebra
14	Geometry and Measurement
15	Geometry and Measurement
16	Algebra
17	Number Sense and Operations
18	Data Analysis
19	Data Analysis
20	Geometry and Measurement
21	Number Sense and Operations
22	Data Analysis
23	Data Analysis
24	Number Sense and Operations
25	Geometry and Measurement

APPENDIX: FORMULAS CHART

Area

Square: $A = \text{side}^2$
Rectangle: $A = \text{length} \times \text{width}$
Parallelogram: $A = \text{base} \times \text{height}$
Triangle: $A = \frac{1}{2} \times \text{base} \times \text{height}$
Trapezoid: $A = \frac{1}{2}(\text{base}_1 + \text{base}_2) \times \text{height}$
Circle: $A = \pi \times \text{radius}^2$; π is approximately equal to 3.14

Circumference

Circle: $C = \pi \times \text{diameter}$; π is approximately equal to 3.14

Distance between Points on a Coordinate Plane

distance between points $= \sqrt{(x_2 - x_1)^2 + (y_2 - y_1)^2}$, where (x_1, y_1) and (x_2, y_2) are two points on the line

Distance Formula

Distance = Rate $\times$ Time

Measures of Central Tendency

Mean = $\frac{(x_1 + x_2 \ldots + x_n)}{n}$, where x's are values for which a mean is desired and n is the total number of values for x

Median: the middle value of an odd number of ordered scores, and halfway between the two middle values of an even number of ordered scores

Perimeter

Square: $P = 4 \times \text{side}$
Rectangle: $P = 2 \times \text{length} + 2 \times \text{width}$
Triangle: $P = \text{side}_1 + \text{side}_2 + \text{side}_3$
Pythagorean Theorem: $a^2 + b^2 = c^2$, where a and b are the legs and c is the hypotenuse of a right triangle

Simple Interest Formula

Interest = Principal $\times$ Rate $\times$ Time

Slope of a Line on a Coordinate Plane

slope of a line = $\frac{(y_2 - y_1)}{(x_2 - x_1)}$, where (x_1, y_1) and (x_2, y_2) are two points on the line

Total Cost

total cost = (number of units) $\times$ (price per unit)

Volume

Cube: $V = \text{edge}^3$
Rectangular solid: $V = \text{length} \times \text{width} \times \text{height}$
Square pyramid: $V = \frac{1}{3} \times (\text{base edge})^2 \times \text{height}$
Cone: $V = \frac{1}{3} \times \pi \times \text{radius}^2 \times \text{height}$; π is approximately equal to 3.14
Cylinder: $V = \pi \times \text{radius}^2 \times \text{height}$; π is approximately equal to 3.14

ADDITIONAL
ONLINE PRACTICE

Whether you need help building basic skills or preparing for an exam, visit LearningExpress Practice Center! Using the code below, you'll be able to access additional online practice. This online practice will also provide you with:

> **Immediate scoring**
> **Detailed answer explanations**
> **A customized diagnostic report that will assess your skills and focus your study**

Log into the LearningExpress Practice Center by using the URL: **www.learnatest.com/practice**

This is your Access Code: **7960**

Follow the steps online to redeem your access code. After you've used your access code to register with the site, you will be prompted to create a username and password. For easy reference, record them here:

Username: _____   **Password:** _____

If you have any questions or problems, please contact LearningExpress customer service at 1-800-295-9556 ext. 2, or e-mail us at **customerservice@learningexpressllc.com**